The
500 BEST-VALUE

WINES *in the* LCBO

UPDATED FIFTH EDITION
WITH OVER 150 NEW WINES

Rod Phillips

20
13

D1205622

whitecap

PUBLISHER   Michael Burch
EDITORS   Lesley Cameron and Theresa Best (2013 edition)
DESIGNER   Grace Partridge
TYPESETTER   Michelle Furbacher

Printed in Canada

⁊❧

Cataloguing in Publication data available from Library and Archives Canada.

ISBN: 978-1-77050-069-3

The publisher acknowledges the financial support of the Government of Canada
through the Canada Book Fund (CBF) and the Province of British Columbia through
the Book Publishing Tax Credit.

12 13 14 15 16   5 4 3 2 1

CONTENTS

Red Wines

PREFACE TO THE 2013 EDITION

This book is a guide to the best-value wines among the wide range available in LCBO (Liquor Control Board of Ontario) stores throughout Ontario. (And if you're not in Ontario, chances are that you'll find many of these wines where you live.) There are so many good- to great-value wines available at reasonable prices in the LCBO that it's a pity not to take advantage of them. If you tend to buy the same couple of wines time after time, this list will help you broaden your horizons and also reduce the financial risk in being adventurous. If you're already adventurous, you're sure to find wines here that you haven't tried.

To compile this list of 500 wines, I tasted nearly all the wines continuously available in the LCBO, and my ratings and reviews point you to wine values and styles you'll easily recognize. Each wine is ranked out of five stars (see How I Rate the Wines on page 4) but I encourage you to read the description of each wine. Stars (like ratings on a 100-point scale) don't tell you what any wine is like when you drink it. I've included some new wines that didn't feature in the 2011 edition of this book. You can identify them easily by their NEW! symbol.

There was no 2012 edition of this book, so this 2013 edition includes many wines that have come onto the LCBO's shelves in the last two years. In that time, some new styles of wine, like those made from the moscato variety, have emerged, and some countries, like Argentina, have increased their representation dramatically. Changes like these are reflected in the range of wines I have reviewed. Conversely, many of the wines in the LCBO have been there for many years. This is not a bad thing, as most of them stay on the shelves because they're good wines, reliable vintage after vintage, and supported by loyal consumers. After re-tasting almost the whole LCBO inventory, I dropped some of these wines, added others and changed some ratings. Although there's not a lot of variation from vintage to vintage in most of the LCBO wines, there is some, and I've made changes accordingly.

Overall, the quality of wines in the LCBO has been rising steadily. The first edition of this book, in 2008, included wines rated from three to five stars. By the 2011 edition, there were very few three-star wines. In this edition, there are none at all. That indicates a steady rise in quality and value. There's just no need to buy mediocre or poor-value wines.

Another difference between this and previous editions, which you may or may not notice, is that I'm using lower case letters for all varieties now. That means we're drinking merlot and chardonnay, for example, instead of Merlot and Chardonnay. Similarly, champagne and bordeaux refer to the wines, while Champagne and Bordeaux are the regions. Why the change? To be honest, it's a personal preference, but if you do any reading about wine you'll probably have noticed several other established wine writers are also committing to lower case these days. The important thing to remember is that it doesn't affect the taste of the wine.

Once again, I thank all the wine agencies and individual wineries, together with their sales, communications and marketing people, for providing me with the wines I tasted for this book.

I also wish to thank the Liquor Control Board of Ontario for inviting me to the regular tastings of Vintages, Vintages Essentials and General Purchase wines.

And it was a pleasure to work with the people at Whitecap Books again: Theresa Best, Lesley Cameron, Michelle Furbacher and Joan Templeton.

I hope you find this book a useful guide to finding wines you enjoy. If you come across a wine that's not in here, but that you think should be included in the next edition, please let me know. You can reach me at rod@rodphillipsonwine.com.

Cheers!

Rod

SOME WINE TRENDS TO WATCH FOR

Tasting almost all the wines in the LCBO has alerted me to a number of trends.

Argentinian malbec continues its roll. But there's a lot of speculation about "The Next Big Red." Could it be bonarda (also from Argentina), syrah (rather than the more fruit-forward style generally labelled 'shiraz') or tempranillo (Spain's signature variety, now planted in many parts of the world)? Maybe pinotage (from South Africa)? Maybe none of these. The preconditions for going big are: there has to be plenty of it (all four of the above qualify), it has to be made in a popular style (all can be) and it has to catch on (we'll see).

The popularity of moscato is building. In 2010–11 it became a big thing in the US, where it drew off many white zinfandel drinkers, and has since made its way into Canada. There are several in this book.

Rosé wines continue to increase in number and popularity. No longer just pink and sweet and dismissively labelled "women's wine," the new breed of varietally labelled rosés tend to be dry and well made. Look for the well-made off-dry styles, too. Starting in spring, the LCBO brings in "seasonal volumes" of rosés that aren't available year-round.

Sparkling wine is finally escaping from the celebration ghetto. People have realized that sparkling wine (including champagne) is not only for anniversaries, weddings, birthdays and the like, but for everyday drinking. As a result, there are more and more sparkling wines available, as the range in this book shows.

"Regionality" is still a buzz word. Wine-producing countries like Australia and Chile want us to think in regional terms, not simply national terms. They want us to go looking for a wine from South Australia, Barossa Valley or Margaret River, and not just "an Australian wine." In this year's list, you'll see more and more wines labelled by specific and smaller regions.

The LCBO has abandoned its ventures into wine packaged in plastic bottles and TetraPak cartons. Glass has won the packaging battle, but the LCBO now mandates a maximum weight for bottles in order to counter a tendency to put some wines in heavy bottles to make them seem weightier in quality. Lighter bottles save energy in transportation and are easier on the backs of LCBO workers.

Critters are on the decline. There are fewer animals, cuddly or otherwise, on wine labels these days. The current tendency is toward labels with more modern, clean designs.

Alcohol levels in wine continue their gentle rise, and levels of 14 percent and 14.5 percent are not uncommon. Although there are some complaints about this, and scattered attempts to bring alcohol levels down, there's no evidence that levels are declining.

HOW I DESCRIBE THE WINES

The common North American way of describing wines is to use fruit, spices and other produce (and things) as references. We've all seen wines described as having aromas and flavours like "red cherry, plum and black pepper, with notes of leather" or "tropical fruit, peach and citrus." I call these "Carmen Miranda" reviews. Sometimes reviewers get even more specific and find flavours such as "damson plum, ripe Red Delicious apples and Bing cherries, with nuances of finely ground green peppercorns."

Research shows that very few people can distinguish these flavours in wine, although it's a skill that many can learn. But even though it is possible to discern these aromas and flavours, no wine ever really tastes primarily like a combination of cherry, plum and black pepper (just imagine it), or of tropical fruit, peach and citrus. There might be hints or reminders of these flavours in the wine, but they're details. Just watch professionals swirling and sniffing (sometimes favouring one nostril over the other), as they strain to pick up and identify the most subtle and fleeting aromas. Focusing on these nuances misses the big picture.

In this book, I focus on the main characteristics of each wine, and on its style: Is it light, medium or full bodied? Is it simple and fruity or well structured? Is it dry, off-dry, sweet or very sweet? Is it tannic or not? Does it have a smooth, tangy, juicy or crisp texture? These are the most important qualities, whether you're looking for a wine to sip on its own or a wine to go with specific food.

Most of us describe wine in these terms. We say we like red wine that's full bodied and rich, white wine that's light and refreshing or rosé that's slightly sweet. And when we're looking for wine to go with dinner, we might think of a heavy red for steak, or a lighter white or crisp rosé for a summer salad.

What we don't look for is a wine with flavours of black plums or raspberries, or notes of red grapefruit, black pepper or honey. And we certainly don't say we love wines with flavours of wet stones, smoky tar or hard-ridden horses—the sorts of descriptions loved by some wine reviewers.

In short, you'll find that the reviews in this book describe wines in the common-sense way in which most people think of them.

HOW I RATE THE WINES

I tasted not only all the wines listed in this book, but about another thousand in addition. They represent the wines available in the LCBO General Purchase and the Vintages Essentials lists. As far as I know, I'm the only person who tastes almost all the LCBO wines in a short period (I do it in five weeks), and this gives me a unique perspective on the LCBO's wines.

I taste the reds at a cool temperature—the way they should be served—and the whites, rosés and sparkling wines chilled, but not cold.

The 500 wines in this book are the ones I consider the best in terms of their intrinsic quality and value. The quality of a wine depends on the balance among its various components (fruit, acidity, alcohol and tannins) and the complexity of its flavours, structure and texture. A wine that's well balanced and very complex scores higher than one with little complexity or poor balance.

All the wines here are good-to-excellent quality, and the five-star rating system reflects their value to the consumer. A $10 wine rated as four-and-a-half stars is better value than a $10 wine rated as three-and-a-half stars. But good value can be found at all price levels. A $30 wine rated as four stars has a quality level that is very good value for its price.

Here's what my star system means:

★ ★ ★ ★ ★   It's hard to imagine better value at this price. This wine is very well balanced and very complex.

★ ★ ★ ★ ½   Excellent value at this price. The wine is well balanced and very complex.

★ ★ ★ ★   Very good value at this price. The wine is well balanced and complex.

★ ★ ★ ½   Above-average value at this price. The wine has fair levels of balance and complexity.

★ ★ ★   Good value at this price. The wine is well made but might be a little unbalanced and might lack much complexity.

HOW TO READ MY REVIEWS

Indicates that the wine is new to this edition.

BRAND OR WINERY

RATING (*out of five*)

GRAPE VARIETY

VINTAGE YEAR

NEW!
★ ★ ★ ★

Graffigna 'Centenario' Reserve Pinot Grigio 2011

SAN JUAN $12.95   164756

[Vintages Essential] Yes, there are Argentinian wines from regions other than Mendoza! This one, from an arid region just to the north of Mendoza, shows lovely fruit flavours and a vibrant and refreshing texture. It's dry and medium bodied, and it's the sort of wine you can enjoy on its own or with food. If you're bringing it to the table, bring along dishes featuring poultry or pork, or cream-based pasta.

NOTES
....
....
....
....
....

[Vintages Essential] *indicates the wine is found in the Vintages section, or at a Vintages store.* [Non-vintage] *indicates that the wine doesn't show a year on its label.*

LCBO PRODUCT CODE

PRICE
(*per 750 mL bottle, unless otherwise indicated*)

REGION

ABOUT THE LCBO

The LCBO (including Vintages, its fine wine arm) sells more than 80 percent of the wine purchased in Ontario, and its wine sales totalled more than $1.6 billion in the 2010/2011 fiscal year. The remaining wine sales are made by winery retail stores, online merchants and importing agents who sell directly to restaurants, bars and individual clients. The LCBO is where most Ontarians shop for wine because it has so many locations and offers the biggest range of imported and Canadian wines in the province.

Critics of the LCBO often complain that its wine selection is too limited, but most consumers find it bewilderingly large. That's why I've written this book. It guides you to the best-value wines on the General Purchase List, which comprises most of the wines in the LCBO. The others are in Vintages stores or Vintages sections of the LCBO. I review some of the wines always available in the Vintages Essentials collection, which numbers about 100.

It can sometimes be a challenge to locate a particular wine in the LCBO. There are more than 600 LCBO stores throughout Ontario, plus more than 200 small agencies in isolated localities, and the range of wine varies widely from outlet to outlet. The main LCBO stores in major cities carry nearly all the LCBO's wines, while others have a more limited selection on hand.

In the unlikely event that you forget to bring this book along when you go wine shopping, you can ask an LCBO Product Consultant for help. They have passed LCBO wine-knowledge examinations and they know the LCBO's inventory well.

If you see a wine in this book that you'd like to try, but you discover it's not in your local LCBO, call the liquor board's helpline at 1-800-ONT-LCBO (1-800-668-5226). An agent will tell you the nearest store that has the wine you're looking for. Alternatively, use the search engine on the LCBO site at lcbo.com to find a wine and identify the LCBO stores that have it.

Bear in mind that the LCBO's inventory is constantly changing. New wines are added and others are dropped. Prices change, too, according to currency exchange fluctuations and other factors. The prices in this book were correct at the time I compiled the list of wines, and include the refundable 20-cent bottle deposit. These are the prices you pay at the till.

The vintages of wines in the LCBO also change, as one vintage sells out and is replaced by the next. You might see a 2010 wine listed here and find that only the 2011 vintage is on the LCBO shelf. For the most part, there is relatively little variation among vintages in the wines on the General Purchase List, and it's safe to go with my reviews and ratings, even when the vintage is different.

BUYING, SERVING & DRINKING WINE: SOME COMMON QUESTIONS

Are wines sealed with a screw cap poorer quality than wines sealed with a cork?
Not at all. In fact, some of the best-known and most reliable producers, like Wolf Blass and Peter Lehmann in Australia, seal all their still wines, including their top brands, with screw caps. There's some scattered debate about the use of screw caps on wines intended for long-term aging, but there's no doubt at all that they are excellent for wines meant to be drunk within five or six years of being made—like all the wines in this book. Natural corks can contain bacteria capable of mildly or seriously tainting wine. They can also produce variability from bottle to bottle, whereas wines sealed with screw caps are almost always more consistent. Are screw caps the last word in wine-bottle closures? Probably not, as experiments with other types of seals are ongoing.

Are wines in boxes or in plastic poorer quality than wines in glass bottles?
There's a common misconception that only inferior wine is sold in boxes (like TetraPak cartons) or bottles made of plastic (such as PET, a food-grade plastic that does not taint the contents). You can't generalize about the quality of wine based on its packaging; after all, there are plenty of poor wines in glass bottles. In practice, though, many producers put their lower-quality wines in boxes or plastic. The only reason why excellent wine might not be sold in such packaging is that there's some question about how long it preserves wine in good condition.

Are more expensive wines better than cheaper ones?
In very broad terms, there is often a relationship between quality and price. High-quality wine demands high-quality grapes (which are often more expensive to grow or buy) and may involve more expense in production, such as the use of oak barrels. But although it's not as easy to find a great wine under $10 or $15 as over $20 or $30, this book shows that there are plenty of high-quality wines at very reasonable prices.

Should I worry about the alcohol level in wine?

By definition, wine contains alcohol. Nearly all of us buy wine not only because we enjoy the flavour and texture, but also for the effects of the alcohol. That said, the level of alcohol—which must be shown on the bottle, and is expressed as a percentage by volume—varies widely. Some whites, like off-dry rieslings, have about 10 percent alcohol, while some reds, notably zinfandels, exceed 14.5 percent. The difference is significant: A glass of 14.5-percent-alcohol wine gives you almost 50 percent more alcohol than the same glass of 10-percent-alcohol wine. Whether that's important depends on the circumstances—for example, how important it is for you to remain alert and unimpaired. As far as your experience of the wine is concerned, high alcohol is not a problem as long as the wine is balanced. If the wine smells of alcohol or if you can feel the warmth of the alcohol as you drink it, it's unbalanced, and the wine is flawed, just as it is when the acidity dominates the fruit or when jammy fruit kills the acidity and leaves the wine flat.

Are wine labels a good guide to what's inside the bottle?

Labels are an important part of marketing wine. Wine is no different from other products, and producers expect that consumers will often be drawn to a particular wine by its packaging—and that usually means the label. Labels can be sophisticated (like those on many expensive and ultra-premium wines), fun (like most of the labels featuring animals) and even provocative (like the Fat Bastard brand). The fact that all are represented in this book shows that there's no necessary link between the label and quality or value. But beyond projecting an image, labels provide consumers with important information. Depending on where the wine is from, the label tells the grape variety (or varieties) used to make the wine and/or where the grapes were grown. The label also tells you the vintage and the alcohol content, and it might give information such as whether the wine is organic, kosher or fair trade. Some of this information might be on a back label, along with a description of the wine, the production process or the producer. But bear in mind that any description of the wine on the back label is written by the producer to promote sales.

Does the serving temperature of wine make any difference?

The serving temperature of wine does matter because it affects qualities in the wine such as flavour and texture (the way the wine feels in your mouth). Too many people (and restaurants) serve white wine too cold and red wine too warm. White wines are refreshing when they're chilled, but most should not be served straight from the fridge. Wine that's too cold has little flavour, so take white wine out of the fridge 15 or 20 minutes before you serve it. Red wine, on the other hand, should be served cooler than it usually is— especially in restaurants where the wine is stored on shelves in the dining room. Red wine should feel cool in your mouth, which means cooler than the 20°c and higher of most homes and restaurants. (The guideline of serving red wine "at room temperature" is not very useful if you like to live in sauna-like temperatures.) If your red wine is too warm, it will feel coarse and flabby and it won't have the refreshing quality that makes wine such an ideal partner for food. To cool red wine that's too warm, put it in the fridge for 15 or 20 minutes before serving. Remember, it's better to serve any wine too cool (but not cold) than too warm; it will warm up quite quickly in your glass.

How many different kinds of wine glasses do I need?

If you look in wine accessory, kitchen and even many department stores, you'll see a wide selection of wine glasses in many different shapes and sizes, often classified by grape variety. Do you really need one glass for chardonnay, another for merlot and another for pinot noir? No, you don't. Although the shape and size of the glass can sometimes highlight the qualities in different wines, you can enjoy nearly all from one or two different glasses. In general, most people prefer to drink wine from finer glasses than from thicker-sided tumblers or glasses. Look for glasses that are wider toward the bottom of the bowl, and fill the glass only to the widest point. That gives room for the aromas to collect. And if you're interested in tasting wine as judges and professionals do, buy some tasting glasses at a wine accessories store. Tasting glasses are smaller than most wine glasses, wide at the bottom and tapered toward the mouth (like the stylized glasses on the cover of this book), and they bring out the aromas and flavours of wines very well. Sparkling wine is frequently served in a tall, slender glass (called a flute) that shows off the bubbles to best effect, but many professionals prefer to drink it from a bigger, wider glass that captures aromas more effectively.

Should I let wine "breathe" before I serve it?

There's a common belief that wine should be opened and left standing to "breathe" for an hour or two before being served. It's based on the theory, which is true, that most wine improves after being exposed to air for a short time. But simply opening a bottle of wine exposes a very small amount of wine (the dime-size surface in the neck of the bottle) to air, and it makes no perceptible difference to the wine. Pouring the wine into glasses as soon as you open the bottle exposes the wine to air far more effectively than letting it stand in the open bottle for hours. You can also decant wine to expose it to air, which leads us to the question . . .

Do I need to decant wine?

There are two reasons to decant wine. The first is to pour off the wine without disturbing the sediment that has collected in the bottom of the bottle to make sure it doesn't get into your glass. Of course, this is necessary only when there's sediment present, and that's rarely the case with wines made for early drinking, like virtually all the wines in this book. The second reason to decant does apply to the wines here—in fact, it applies to any wine, whether it's red, white or rosé—and that's to expose the wine to some air before you drink it. This is more accurately called "aerating" than "decanting," and it generally improves the aromas, flavours and texture of the wine, and therefore its overall quality. You needn't buy an expensive decanter (there are many on the market for less than $15), but look for one with a broad mouth and a wide bottom. If you don't have a decanter to hand but want to aerate a bottle of wine, pour it into a clean bottle (or a pitcher) and then back into the original bottle once or twice.

What do I do with leftover wine?

Opened wine lasts longer if you keep it in the refrigerator and longer still if you keep exposure to air to a minimum. Just re-corking or screwing the cap back on a half-finished bottle leaves the wine exposed to a lot of air, so it's better to pour leftover wine into a smaller container, like a clean half-bottle, where there's little or no air between the surface of the wine and the top of the bottle. If you're keeping a half-full bottle, store it standing up, rather than on its side, so that the surface exposed to air is minimal. Kept in the fridge like this, leftover wine should be good for at least two or three days. If you have leftover sparkling wine, use the same re-sealer as you'd use for a bottle of carbonated soft drink.

Does wine improve with age? Should I have a wine cellar?

While some wines are made for aging, the bulk of the world's wine is made for drinking as soon as it's released for sale. It will not improve with age, but it will eventually deteriorate and become undrinkable. Most consumers buy wine as they need it, but there's no reason why you shouldn't keep a number of bottles of wine on hand for emergencies. For that purpose, you don't need a proper cellar with controlled temperature and humidity, but your wine will keep best if it's in a dark, cool place (ideally between 10°C and 15°C). The corner of a basement, a closet or the space under the stairs might be suitable, but a kitchen counter, where the wine will be exposed to light and heat, is not. Wine kept in too-warm conditions develops a "stewed" flavour. If you do want to store a few dozen or more bottles of wine so that they improve over a longer term, check the Internet or a wine accessory store for information on wine cabinets or how to build a wine cellar.

MATCHING WINE & FOOD

Matching food with wine is not nearly as difficult as many people think—or are led to think by too many wine professionals who make it sound like rocket science. Ignore the complicated treatises that tell you that a smoky note in the wine echoes a hint of smoke in a dish. Similarly, ignore the food and wine matching guides and apps that tell you to pair this food with that wine. Both food and wine vary widely—there's no one chicken curry and no one pinot gris—and you're better off following your own common sense.

A pairing should enhance your enjoyment of both the food and the wine. Avoid a pairing where one overwhelms or interferes with your enjoyment of the other. For example, a full-flavoured wine will smother food that has delicate flavours, and sweet food can make dry wines taste sour. The best pairing is one that leaves the food tasting the way the cook intended and the wine the way the winemaker planned.

Matching wine and food should be fun. Each of the reviews in this book includes a food match that works well, but don't take them too literally. Each suggestion represents a style. A wine that goes with beef will almost always team equally well with lamb and other red meats, and one that pairs successfully with chicken will also marry happily with turkey. Here are some guidelines:

- Match heavier dishes (like red meat and hearty meat or vegetable stews) with medium- to full-bodied wines, and lighter dishes (like salads and white fish) with light- to medium-bodied wines. The weight of food often comes from sauces. White fish alone is light, but a cream sauce makes it heavier.

- Focus on the styles of the entire dish, not just the main item. The overall flavour of unseasoned roast chicken is mild. But chicken in a rich, spicy tomato sauce has more complexity.

- Herbs and spices give a richer and more complex texture to food. Barbecued pork has more complexity than unseasoned pork, for example, and a wine that pairs well with richly flavoured food will match it better.

- Focus on the style of the wine, not only its colour. For the purpose of matching food, a full-bodied, rich, oaked chardonnay might have more in common with a red wine than with a light-bodied, delicate white.

ARGENTINA

ARGENTINA IS THE FIFTH-LARGEST wine producer in the world. It has only in the last ten years become a major wine exporter, but it quickly earned a reputation for producing quality wines at prices that offer very good value. Although better known for its red wines (especially malbec), Argentina produces many excellent whites. One of the most interesting white grapes is torrontés, which has become the country's signature white variety. It generally shows pungent aromas and a crisp, refreshing texture. Other whites are made from popular varieties like chardonnay and pinot grigio.

Most Argentinian wine is labelled by the sprawling Mendoza region, although some is starting to be labelled by some of the smaller sub-regions. Other important wine regions are San Juan, Salta/Cafayate in the north and Patagonia in the south.

Argento Pinot Grigio 2011

★ ★ ★ ½

MENDOZA $9.95 620492

Wine has been made in Argentina (and in Mendoza) since the 1500s, but the attention given to pinot grigio is much more recent. This is a nice example that gets away from the common fruity style and shows a texture that's crisp and refreshing, and in many ways better with food. Look for well-defined flavours and a dry and zesty texture, and serve it with slightly spicy seafood.

NOTES

....

....

....

....

FuZion 'Alta' Torrontés/Pinot Grigio 2011

★ ★ ★ ★

MENDOZA $8.95 168419

The torrontés (pronounced to-ron-TESS) variety deserves to be much better known and appreciated, and maybe harnessing it to pinot grigio will help. The result here is a richly aromatic wine showing lovely concentrated flavours that are defined and quite complex. It's zesty and fresh, and an excellent choice for spicy Asian-influenced dishes that feature pork, poultry or tofu.

NOTES

....

....

....

....

Graffigna 'Centenario' Reserve Pinot Grigio 2011

NEW!
★ ★ ★ ★

SAN JUAN $12.95 164756

Yes, there are Argentinian wines from regions other than Mendoza! This one, from an arid region just to the north of Mendoza, shows lovely fruit flavours and a vibrant and refreshing texture. It's dry and medium bodied, and it's the sort of wine you can enjoy on its own or with food. If you're bringing it to the table, bring along dishes featuring poultry or pork, or cream-based pasta.

NOTES

....

....

....

....

NEW!
★ ★ ★ ½

Las Moras Chardonnay 2010

SAN JUAN$12.45270025

The San Juan wine region, Argentina's second most important, is a virtual desert. This chardonnay doesn't have a lot of complexity, but it's nicely made and goes very well with roasted or grilled poultry and pork. It also has the fruitiness to extend to lightly spicy dishes. Look for a round, smooth texture and good acidity.

NOTES

....

....

....

....

★ ★ ★ ★

Lurton Pinot Gris 2011

VALLE DE UCO, MENDOZA$11.75656746

Lurton is an unusual company in that it makes wine under the same name in many countries. This pinot gris from its winery in Mendoza delivers quite delicious and intense aromas and flavours. It's plush, mouth filling and quite stylish, and has food-friendly edginess. It's a terrific choice for sipping on its own or drinking with spicy seafood and chicken or much Asian cuisine.

NOTES

....

....

....

....

AUSTRALIA

AUSTRALIA GRABBED THE ATTENTION of international wine drinkers in the 1990s, and still has a good grip. Although better known for red wine, especially shiraz, it produces a wide range of whites, too. The most common white variety in Australia is chardonnay, and it accounts for most of the country's white wine exports, but others (such as the popular semillon/sauvignon blanc blend) also cross the Pacific Ocean.

The regional designation often found on Australian wine labels is South Eastern Australia, a huge zone that includes more than 90 percent of Australia's wine production and most of its designated wine regions. But Australian wineries are now stressing the importance of region, rather than simply grape variety, in understanding their wines. In this list of Australian whites, you'll find wines from well-known regions such as South Australia and the Barossa Valley, but also from lesser-known areas such as Clare Valley, Pemberton and Frankland River.

NEW!
★ ★ ★ ★

Clare Hills Riesling 2009

CLARE VALLEY $15.40   215111

Clare Valley, in South Australia, is well known for its riesling, and this
bottle will help you understand why. It delivers a texture that's vibrant
and bracing thanks to the broad seam of bright acidity that underpins the
lovely, succulent, ripe fruit. Fruity and just off-dry, it's great to drink on
its own, but it also goes beautifully with spicy seafood, pork, chicken and
tofu dishes, whether or not they're inspired by Asian cuisine.

NOTES

....

....

....

....

NEW!
★ ★ ★ ½

De Bortoli 'Family Selection' Traminer Riesling 2009

SOUTH EASTERN AUSTRALIA $12.95   207381

This blend of gewürztraminer (in the name, shortened to Traminer)
and riesling makes for an attractive white with bright and pungent fruit
flavours (think gewürztraminer) and vibrant, juicy acidity (think riesling).
It's a very good choice for sipping on its own, enjoying as an aperitif or
serving with a wide spectrum of spicy appetizers and dishes, like many in
Thai cuisine.

NOTES

....

....

....

....

NEW!
★ ★ ★ ★ ½

Fifth Leg Semillon/Sauvignon Blanc 2011

WESTERN AUSTRALIA $15.95   212613

The semillon/sauvignon blanc combination is a classic from Bordeaux.
However, Western Australia produces a lovely white that's substantial and
crisp, and that makes an excellent pairing with grilled white fish, seafood,
shellfish and many curried dishes. The flavours are richly textured and the
texture itself is both solid and vibrantly mouth-watering.

NOTES

....

....

....

....

....

★ ★ ★ ½

Hardys 'Stamp of Australia' Riesling/Gewürztraminer 2011

SOUTH EASTERN AUSTRALIA $8.95   448548

This is a medium-dry (meaning slightly sweet) blend that combines the strengths of the two grape varieties: the crisp texture of riesling and the rich, pungent notes of gewürztraminer. Overall, it's attractive, with bright and concentrated flavours and a refreshing texture. It's medium bodied and goes well with spicy Asian food, so try it next time you get Thai takeout.

NOTES

....

....

....

....

NEW!
★ ★ ★ ½

Jacob's Creek Moscato 2011

AUSTRALIA $10.95   265157

One of the first ripples of what will probably be a wave of moscatos in the LCBO, this is a frizzante (very slightly sparkling) white, a slightly sweet wine in a style the winemaker describes as "happy, fun and upfront." It's light and cheerful—an easy wine to sip on its own, but also up to the challenge of mildly spicy foods.

NOTES

....

....

....

....

....

NEW!
★ ★ ★ ★ ½

Jacob's Creek Reserve Riesling 2010

BAROSSA VALLEY $14.95   212704

Most of the grapes were grown in the higher altitudes of the Eden Valley, a sub-region of Barossa, where they picked up the juicy acidity you can feel when you sip this delicious wine. With its focused fruit flavours and that bright juiciness, it's a natural for fatty things like oysters and smoked salmon, but it also stretches to sushi and many Asian dishes.

NOTES

....

....

....

....

Lindemans 'Bin 65' Chardonnay 2011

★ ★ ★ ½

SOUTH EASTERN AUSTRALIA $10.95   142117

Bin 65 was designed specifically for the Canadian market because of the popularity of chardonnay here. Launched in 1985, it quickly became a global icon. Year after year, it delivers solid, ripe fruit flavours, a clean, smooth and slightly edgy texture, and good balance. It isn't too much of anything but has enough of everything to make it a versatile food wine. Drink it with roast pork or chicken.

NOTES

NEW!

McWilliam's 'Hanwood Estate' Chardonnay 2009

★ ★ ★ ★ ½

SOUTH EASTERN AUSTRALIA $13.95   657934

This medium-bodied, premium chardonnay gets marks for elegance, in addition to its other positive qualities. It delivers lovely, rich, complex flavours with a subtle hint of oak, and everything is lifted by the remarkably refreshing and clean texture. It's fruity but dry, and it's an excellent choice when you're serving chicken, fish, pork or perhaps even seafood in a cream sauce.

NOTES

NEW!

McWilliam's 'Hanwood Estate' Moscato

★ ★ ★ ½

SOUTH EASTERN AUSTRALIA $13.95   212696

[Non-vintage] This is a good choice for the summer patio. It's low in alcohol (a mere 6 percent), has a spritzy texture and is quite sweet, although less so if you chill it down to highlight the acidity. It's a wine for sipping on its own, but the sweetness also allows you to pair it with hot and spicy foods.

NOTES

Penfolds 'Koonunga Hill' Chardonnay 2011

★ ★ ★ ★ ½

SOUTH EASTERN AUSTRALIA $14.95   321943

Dr. Christopher Penfold started making wine in Australia in the 1840s and prescribed it to his settler patients for the anemia that many of them suffered after their long voyage from Britain. Now we drink it for pleasure, and you can certainly enjoy the intense, ripe fruit flavours in this chardonnay. It's medium bodied and very well balanced, and has a rich, attractive texture. Drink it with roast pork or turkey.

NOTES

....

....

....

....

NEW!
★ ★ ★ ★

Peter Lehmann Barossa Blonde 2009

BAROSSA VALLEY $14.95   197871

The Blonde in question is the Queen of Clubs who appears on all Lehmann labels. (Check out peterlehmannwines.com for the full story.) Here she presents lovely rich, bright and pungent fruit flavours, with a splash of vibrant acidity. This is a crisp and substantial wine you can drink on its own or pair with seafood and many not-too-spicy Asian dishes.

NOTES

....

....

....

....

....

NEW!
★ ★ ★ ★

Shingleback 'Haycutters' Sauvignon Blanc/Semillon 2009

ADELAIDE HILLS / MCLAREN VALE $17.95   207365

This blend brings together the fruit and vibrancy of sauvignon blanc and the rounder texture of semillon. Originally from Bordeaux, the combination has been popularized in Australia with fine examples like this. Here you'll find solid fruit flavours with good concentration harnessed to bright acidity, and a crisp yet full texture. It's a great partner for rich fish, seafood, poultry and pork dishes.

NOTES

....

....

....

....

NEW!
★ ★ ★ ★

Tic Tok Chardonnay 2009

MUDGEE / PEMBERTON $14.95   187104

The grapes that made this wine grew on opposite sides of Australia, in Mudgee (New South Wales) and Pemberton (Western Australia). They've come together in more ways than one, and here they present harmonized and finely balanced flavours and textures. Look for lovely fruit flavours with a hint of oak, and a plush but fresh texture. It's a great choice for roast chicken, pork and seared scallops.

NOTES
....
....
....
....

NEW!
★ ★ ★ ★ ½

Tic Tok Sauvignon Blanc 2009

PEMBERTON / FRANKLAND RIVER / MUDGEE

$14.95   187039

The great-great-grandfather of the owner of this winery was a convict who was transported to Australia in 1815 and later pardoned, thanks to his skills as a clockmaker. His descendants have proven skilled in winemaking, as the Tic Tok range shows. This sauvignon blanc shows lovely, plush fruit and crisp, zesty acidity. It's an excellent wine for seafood and white fish dishes, as well as for medium-hot curries.

NOTES
....
....
....

★ ★ ★ ★

Wolf Blass 'Yellow Label' Chardonnay 2011

SOUTH AUSTRALIA $15.00   226860

Wolf Blass 'Yellow Label' cabernet sauvignon was Wolfie's first big hit in Ontario, and now the LCBO shelves have more of his mellow-yellow labels. This is a big chardonnay—fruit forward and the sort of chard that has wide appeal. What gives it quality and value is the complexity of the flavours and the refreshing texture, which makes this a great choice for fish, chicken or pork dishes.

NOTES
....
....
....
....

★ ★ ★

Wyndham Estate 'Bin 222' Chardonnay 2009

SOUTH EASTERN AUSTRALIA $12.50   93401

So many chardonnays . . . and yet some manage to stand out from the crowd. This is one. You'll find the first thing you notice is the smoothness of the texture. The wine seems to glide effortlessly across your palate, filling your mouth with concentrated and nuanced flavours as it does so. For all that, it's more than just fruity, and it has all the refreshing texture needed for chicken, salmon, turkey and pork.

NOTES

....

....

....

....

NEW!
★ ★ ★ ★ ½

Yalumba 'Y Series' Riesling 2010

SOUTH AUSTRALIA $14.95   212753

This very compelling riesling is a study in balance—the balance of fruit and acidity. There's a lot of luscious sweetness and complexity in the ripe fruit flavours, but they're complemented by a seam of bright, mouth-watering and juicy acidity that makes you want to go back for more. And why wouldn't you? This is a great choice for dishes that are moderately spicy, so try it with Asian cuisine.

NOTES

....

....

....

....

AUSTRIA

AUSTRIAN WINE IS BECOMING better known outside Europe, largely because of white wines made from the grüner veltliner grape variety. The other major white grape is riesling. The largest region is Niederösterreich (Lower Austria), which includes well-known appellations such as Kamptal, Kremstal and Wachau.

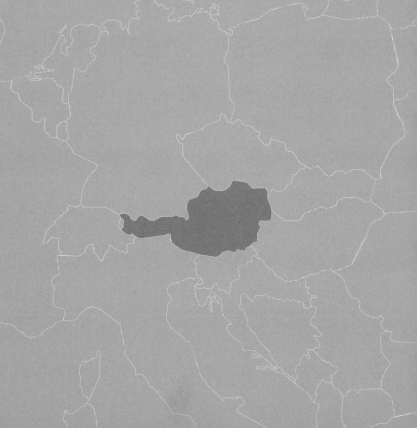

Grooner Grüner Veltliner 2010

★ ★ ★ ½

NIEDERÖSTERREICH $13.35   168625

Although the brand of this wine is a bit of a groaner, Grüner Veltliner has become Austria's signature white wine. It is generally—like this one—made in an easy-drinking style that pairs successfully with food. Here you'll find nicely concentrated, modestly complex flavours paired with crisp, fresh acidity. It's a very good choice for white fish, seafood, chicken and pork.

NOTES

....

....

....

....

BRITISH COLUMBIA

BRITISH COLUMBIA'S WINERIES produce many quality and value-priced white wines, but you won't find very many on LCBO shelves. Don't blame the LCBO. The reason is that British Columbians love their wine and drink most of what's made in their province. Much of the rest is sold in western Canada and in the US states to the south of British Columbia, rather than shipped all the way to Ontario.

The Vintners Quality Alliance (VQA) classification on British Columbia wine labels means that the grapes were grown in the region specified and that the wine has been tested and tasted by a panel. VQA certification is optional.

Mission Hill Reserve Chardonnay 2010

★ ★ ★ ★ ½

VQA OKANAGAN VALLEY $19.95   645004

[Vintages Essential] Mission Hill is the Okanagan Valley's iconic winery, a tourist destination that attracts crowds to see its architecture and its site, and to taste its well-made wines. This chardonnay is rich and elegant with intense, upfront fruit flavours, and a smooth, mouth-filling texture. It's nicely balanced with the crispness needed to make it work well with food. Try it with the quintessential BC grilled salmon.

NOTES

....

....

....

....

CALIFORNIA

A WIDE RANGE OF WHITE GRAPES grows in California's vineyards, but the state is best known for chardonnay, its most popular and widely planted variety. Still, don't overlook other quality whites, especially pinot grigio and sauvignon blanc. Napa Valley is California's most famous region but others, like Sonoma County and Central Coast, as well as smaller appellations like Paso Robles and Lodi, are becoming better known. Many California white wines in this book are designated simply "California," which means that producers can source grapes from any region throughout the state.

Beringer 'Founders' Estate' Chardonnay 2010

★ ★ ★ ★ ½

CALIFORNIA $17.95 634230

The "founders" here are the Beringer boys, brothers Jacob and Frederick, who founded the winery in the 1870s. They'd be proud of this chardonnay, which delivers so well in every respect. The flavours are rich, well defined and complex, while the texture is plush, smooth, mouth filling and refreshing. The combination is a winner that you'll enjoy with richer chicken, pork and seafood dishes.

NOTES

....

....

....

....

Beringer 'Founders' Estate' Pinot Grigio 2010

★ ★ ★ ★ ½

CALIFORNIA $17.95 45641

This is a delicious pinot grigio that delivers real stylishness and elegance. The flavours are well defined with both concentration and delicacy, and the texture shows a beautiful balance of acidity and fruit. It's silky smooth and has a refreshing quality that suits food, although you could savour it on its own, too. If you're thinking of eating, serve it with a delicately spiced Thai dish.

NOTES

....

....

....

....

Beringer 'Stone Cellars' Chardonnay 2007

NEW!
★ ★ ★ ½

CALIFORNIA $13.95 606806

'Stone Cellars' refers to the cellars carved into the cliff face at the Beringer winery in the late nineteenth century. They provided the coolness and humidity needed for aging wine in barrels. This is a chardonnay made in a popular style. It has quite rich, luscious and fruity flavours, and a texture that's mouth filling, smooth and well balanced. Dry and medium weight, it's a good wine for drinking with roasted or grilled chicken or pork.

NOTES

....

....

....

....

NEW!
★ ★ ★ ★ ½

Bonterra Chardonnay 2010

MENDOCINO COUNTY $18.95   342436

Bonterra grows its grapes organically: without the use of chemical fertilizers, pesticides or any other chemical treatment. Whether or not it shows in your experience of the wine is debatable, but there's no debate that this is a fine chardonnay. It combines power (intense fruit flavours) with finesse (a refined and balanced texture), and it's a great choice if you're having chicken, pork or white fish.

NOTES

....

....

....

....

....

NEW!
★ ★ ★ ½

Entwine Pinot Grigio 2010

CALIFORNIA $14.95   272344

Entwining, says the back label, involves pairing food and wine. This wine "entwines" with many spicy Asian dishes, as well as seafood and baked ham. The flavours are bright and vibrant, and they're supported by good acidity that morphs into a texture that's crisp and clean.

NOTES

....

....

....

....

....

NEW!
★ ★ ★ ★

Hahn Chardonnay 2008

MONTEREY COUNTY $16.95   234393

Hahn means "rooster" in German, and the producers can certainly crow about this lovely chardonnay. It delivers quite rich, complex flavours, with a hint of oakiness, and pairs them with bright acidity that gives the wine a juicy texture. Solid and light on its feet . . . a very good combination. Drink this with roasted chicken or pork, or grilled chicken or white fish.

NOTES

....

....

....

....

J. Lohr 'Riverstone' Chardonnay 2010

★ ★ ★ ★ ★

ARROYO SECO $18.95 258699

[Vintages Essential] This is a stylish and opulent chardonnay from the little-known Arroyo Seco wine region in central California. Here you get plush, ripe and multi-faceted fruit flavours that sit harmoniously with a texture that's full, round and refreshing. It's dry and medium bodied, and very well balanced. Enjoy this with herbed roast chicken, grilled salmon or pork tenderloin, or seared scallops or lobster.

NOTES

Montevina Pinot Grigio 2010

NEW!
★ ★ ★ ½

CALIFORNIA $14.95 237750

There's lots of sweet, ripe fruit in this pinot grigio. It doesn't offer too much complexity, but it's attractive in flavour and the fruit is balanced by clean, crisp acidity. This dry, medium-weight white goes well with many styles of food. Try it with roast chicken or pork, white fish and seafood, and with not-too-spicy dishes.

NOTES

Painter Bridge Chardonnay 2010

NEW!
★ ★ ★ ★

CALIFORNIA $13.55 230516

There's loads of flavour in this concentrated and medium-plus-bodied chardonnay, and some evidence of oak. Then the acidity kicks in and delivers a vibrant juiciness that brings the intensity to heel. Overall, it's an attractive style that goes well with a variety of foods. Try it with grilled or roasted chicken or pork, with creamy pasta, or with seafood and white fish.

NOTES

Robert Mondavi 'Private Selection' Chardonnay 2010

★ ★ ★ ★ ½
CALIFORNIA $16.95   379180

Try this on any chardonnay-skeptic—you know, the people who loudly declare that they don't like chardonnay, as if it's something to be proud of. Chardonnay comes in so many styles, and this is a particularly attractive one. It's medium to full bodied, and has a smooth texture and lovely concentrated flavours. It's a versatile, fruit-filled chardonnay that goes as well with roasted chicken as with grilled salmon.

NOTES
....
....
....
....

Robert Mondavi 'Private Selection' Sauvignon Blanc 2010

★ ★ ★ ½
CALIFORNIA $16.95   405753

This is a very good sauvignon blanc for drinking with food, and I'd be happy to drink it with white fish, seafood with a spritz of lemon or even lemon chicken, for that matter. It doesn't have the flavour power of some sauvignon blancs (like many from New Zealand) but it's very solid, attractive and well balanced, and has the refreshing and clean texture you want in this variety.

NOTES
....
....
....
....

Seaglass Sauvignon Blanc 2010

★ ★ ★ ★
SANTA BARBARA COUNTY $13.95   173575

There's a lot to like in this sauvignon blanc from southern California. It's very refreshing, with brisk acidity etching its way into the concentrated, focused and somewhat pungent flavours. It's dry and well balanced, and has the stuff to go well with seafood, shellfish and white fish, as well as with chicken and creamy pasta dishes.

NOTES
....
....
....
....

★ ★ ★ ★ ½

Toasted Head Chardonnay 2010
CALIFORNIA $17.95   694341

[Vintages Essential] 'Toasted Head' refers to the practice of charring the insides of barrels. Often the ends (heads) are not toasted, but in the barrels used to age this chardonnay, they were. This is a bold and assertive chardonnay with intense flavours and a round texture, but it carries the liveliness needed to pair well with food. Drink it with grilled salmon, pork tenderloin or herbed roast chicken.

NOTES
....
....
....
....

★ ★ ★ ★ ½

Wente 'Morning Fog' Chardonnay 2010
LIVERMORE VALLEY / SAN FRANCISCO BAY $16.95   175430

The morning fog is important to many California wine regions. It swirls up the river valleys at dawn and keeps the vines cool until it eventually dissipates in late morning or early afternoon. The results are chardonnays like this that retain wonderful freshness of flavour and texture, while having concentrated fruit and a round, silky mouth feel. It's a delicious wine with chicken, turkey or pork.

NOTES
....
....
....
....

NEW!
★ ★ ★ ½

Woodbridge Moscato 2010
CALIFORNIA $11.95   199216

Among the moscatos currently in the LCBO, this is one of the sweetest. It has all the hallmarks of the popular style—sweetness, aromatics, fruitiness and decent acidity—but the sweetness here stands out. If you like sipping sweet wines, this is for you, but many more people will find it a good pairing with rich foods like foie gras and with spicy Asian dishes.

NOTES
....
....
....
....
....

Woodbridge Pinot Grigio 2010

CALIFORNIA $11.95   379180

A few years ago, it seemed that pinot grigio (pinot gris) might overtake chardonnay as the most popular white. It didn't happen, but there's no shortage of pinot grigio around. There's plenty of sweet, ripe fruit in this one, complemented by a clean and tangy texture. It's very dry, medium weight and nicely balanced, and it goes well with a range of food: chicken, pork, spicy dishes, seafood, white fish . . .

NOTES

....

....

....

....

CHILE

ALTHOUGH CHILE IS BETTER KNOWN for its red wines, many of its whites offer great quality and value. The warm growing conditions in most of Chile's wine regions have led many producers to seek out cooler areas (like the Casablanca Valley) and to plant white grape vines at higher (and cooler) altitudes. The main white varieties planted are chardonnay and sauvignon blanc, but there are others.

Designated Chilean wine regions are indicated by the initials DO (*Denominación de Origen*).

NEW!
★★★ ½

35° South Reserva Sauvignon Blanc 2010

DO CURICÓ / ELQUI VALLEY $12.85   170001

From vines growing in two of Chile's more remote wine regions, this sauvignon blanc delivers concentrated and pungent flavours underpinned by a seam of rich, acute acidity. Fruit and acid are in good balance, and make for a zesty texture that suits the wine well for seafood, shellfish and white fish, but it also goes well with poultry and with many cream-based dishes.

NOTES
....
....
....
....

NEW!
★★★ ½

Adobe Reserva Sauvignon Blanc 2011

DO CASABLANCA VALLEY $12.95   266049

From one of Chile's premium sauvignon blanc regions, this shows lovely vibrant fruit that's underpinned by a seam of crisp, zesty acidity. It's dry and medium weight, and delivers a decent level of complexity. It's a very good choice for white fish and seafood and fresh lemon juice, and it also goes well with mild curries.

NOTES
....
....
....
....
....

★★★★ ½

Caliterra Reserva Sauvignon Blanc 2011

DO CASABLANCA VALLEY $8.95   275909

The regions generally considered best for sauvignon blanc are the Loire Valley in France and Marlborough in New Zealand, but Chile produces well-priced competition. This one, made from grapes grown in one of Chile's prime sauvignon blanc regions, has a crisp, refreshing texture and vibrant, fresh fruit flavours. It's medium bodied and goes well with a goat cheese salad or with fish or seafood juiced with fresh lemon.

NOTES
....
....
....
....

Casillero del Diablo Reserva Sauvignon Blanc 2011

★ ★ ★ ½

DO CENTRAL VALLEY $10.95   678641

This has everything you want from a straightforward, well-made, inexpensive sauvignon blanc. It shows flavours that are concentrated and nicely complex, and a texture that's both tangy and refreshing. Dry and medium bodied, it goes well with white fish and seafood with a squeeze of lemon, and it's an excellent party wine when you're serving spicy appetizers.

NOTES

....

....

....

....

Cono Sur Chardonnay 2011

NEW!
★ ★ ★ ★

DO SAN ANTONIO VALLEY $11.95   230565

This is an organic wine, meaning that no chemicals are used in the vineyards or winery. The vineyards are in the cool San Antonio Valley, where the sun ripens the grapes and the cool air allows the acidity to develop. The result is a lovely, refreshing, well-balanced wine with sweet fruit flavours and good complexity. Enjoy this with poultry, white fish, seafood and pork.

NOTES

....

....

....

....

Cono Sur Viognier 2010

★ ★ ★ ★ ★

DO COLCHAGUA VALLEY $9.95   64287

You can make this your go-to white when you're eating spicy Thai or Indian dishes. It has rich, delicious, sweet fruit flavours and a refreshing texture, all of which tend to tame the spiciness a little without interfering with the flavours. Viognier is an under-appreciated variety, and this one comes from a winery that has pioneered many sustainable practices in its vineyards.

NOTES

....

....

....

....

Errazuriz 'Estate Reserva' Chardonnay 2011

★ ★ ★ ★

CASABLANCA VALLEY $11.95   318741

Chile's Casablanca Valley appellation is an area where the vines are cooled by breezes from the nearby Pacific Ocean. The coolness promotes the development of acidity and the sunshine ripens the grapes—and one result is this chardonnay. Here you find sweet, ripe fruit—well focused and concentrated—and fresh acidity, working harmoniously together. It's great with poultry, pork and white fish.

NOTES

....

....

....

....

J. Bouchon Sauvignon Blanc 2011

★ ★ ★ ½

DO MAULE VALLEY $9.25   631749

There's a sort of irony here in that *bouchon* is the French word for "cork" and this wine is sealed with a screw cap. The wine itself has good, concentrated, ripe flavours, and they flow in on a texture that's quite round, but tangy and crisp. It's a refreshing white that goes well with grilled seafood and white fish (with lemon) and also with warm goat cheese salads.

NOTES

....

....

....

....

Maipo Reserva Chardonnay 2011

NEW!
★ ★ ★ ★ ½

CASABLANCA VALLEY $13.95   270009

This gets a bit confusing: Maipo Valley is a wine region in Chile, but this Maipo-brand chardonnay is sourced from Casablanca. It's all to the good, though, because Casablanca's sunny, cool conditions produced this lovely wine. Look for quite rich flavours with a touch of oak, zesty acidity to provide balance, and a refreshing, food-friendly texture. Enjoy it with pork, poultry and grilled white fish.

NOTES

....

....

....

....

Santa Rita '120' Sauvignon Blanc 2011

★ ★ ★ ★

DO CENTRAL VALLEY $10.95   23606

Sauvignon blanc has been "discovered" in the last ten years and this has led to plantings in many different conditions. In turn, several different styles have emerged, and this example from Santa Rita sits in the middle ground. Dry and very well balanced, it delivers full flavours and retains the tangy zestiness that makes sauvignon blanc such a great wine when you're having white fish and seafood.

NOTES

....

....

....

....

Santa Rita Reserva Chardonnay 2010

★ ★ ★ ★ ½

DO CASABLANCA VALLEY $13.95   348359

Santa Rita is one of Chile's established wineries, but it doesn't rest on its well-deserved laurels. There's real quality in this Casablanca chardonnay, grown in a relatively recently developed cool region that produces fresh, crisp, well-focused wines. The flavours are concentrated, the texture tangy and refreshing, and the overall image very attractive. Serve it with pork tenderloin or roast chicken.

NOTES

....

....

....

....

Santa Rita Reserva Sauvignon Blanc 2011

★ ★ ★ ★

DO CASABLANCA VALLEY $13.95   275677

Sauvignon blanc is popular because of its characteristic crispness and clean, pungent notes, which it develops when the grapes grow in cooler areas. The vineyards in Chile's Casablanca Valley are fanned by cold breezes that blow in from the Pacific Ocean early each afternoon. They give zesty texture and lovely flavours to this sauvignon blanc, which is a great choice for fish or seafood with a squeeze of lemon.

NOTES

....

....

....

FRANCE

THE NUMEROUS FRENCH WINE REGIONS produce whites from many different varieties of grapes. Some regions are closely tied to specific grapes—like Burgundy to chardonnay, and Sancerre to sauvignon blanc—but others are not. You'll find a wide range of varieties and styles in this list.

French wine labels display a few terms worth knowing. Wines labelled *Appellation d'Origine Contrôlée* (abbreviated AOC in this book) or *Appellation d'Origine Protégée* (AOP) are wines in the highest quality classification in France. They're made under tight rules that regulate such aspects as the grape varieties that can be used in each region.

Wines labelled *Vin de Pays* or IGP (*Indication Géographique Protégée*) are regional wines made with fewer restrictions. They must be good quality, but producers have much more flexibility in the grapes they can use and how much wine they can make. *Vins de Pays d'Oc* (the ancient region of Occitanie) are by far the most important of the *Vins de Pays* wines.

NEW!
★ ★ ★ ½

Baron Philippe de Rothschild Viognier 2010

IGP PAYS D'OC $10.95   619221

Viognier (pronounced vee-OH-nyay) is widely grown in southern France, and is sometimes blended with syrah (shiraz) to add complexity. Here you get a look at the variety on its own. It has restrained and decently complex flavours, with an attractive (really!) hint of bitterness at the end. With crisp acidity, it's a good partner for slightly spicy dishes and for roast chicken.

NOTES

....

....

....

....

★ ★ ★ ★

Bouchard Père & Fils Mâcon-Lugny Saint-Pierre 2009

AOC MÂCON-LUGNY $14.95   61573

This is from a designated area in the Mâcon region, in southern Burgundy. Made from 100 percent chardonnay, it's an elegant wine delivering nicely concentrated flavours that are soft and stylish. The texture is quite rich and creamy, with a seam of acidity that adds a refreshing note. This is an excellent wine for grilled salmon, and for meats like chicken, turkey and pork.

NOTES

....

....

....

....

★ ★ ★ ★

Bouchard Père & Fils Petit Chablis 2010

AOC PETIT CHABLIS $19.95   61466

Petit Chablis is one of the appellations (designated regions) of the broader Chablis region, and it's often dismissed, partly because of the low minimum alcohol (this one is 12 percent). But this is ideal if you want a lower-alcohol wine, especially in the heat of summer. The flavours are restrained and defined. It's refreshing and a very good match for chicken, white fish and seafood.

NOTES

....

....

....

....

★ ★ ★ ★ ★
Bouchard Père & Fils Pouilly-Fuissé 2010
AOC POUILLY-FUISSÉ $26.90   66580

Pouilly-Fuissé is a prestigious region in southern Burgundy that produces only white wine and grows only chardonnay. Don't expect to see this labelled as a chardonnay, though, as the regional name is a selling point. It's gorgeous and stylish, with pure and nuanced flavours and a beautifully smooth and clean texture. Medium weight and dry, it's a great choice for poultry, pork, fish or seafood.

NOTES
....
....
....
....

NEW!
★ ★ ★ ★ ½
Domaine des Aspes Viognier 2009
VIN DE PAYS D'OC $15.95   712638

This is an elegant white that shows understated and nuanced flavours, rather than the more obvious aromatics and flavours associated with many other viogniers. Underpinning the flavour profile is a broad seam of crisp acidity that's well integrated into the fruit and makes for a freshness that's not immediately identifiable as acid. This viognier goes well with poultry, pork and many white fish and seafood dishes.

NOTES
....
....
....
....

NEW!
★ ★ ★ ★ ½
Domaine Laroche 'Saint Martin' Chablis 2010
AOC CHABLIS $21.95   289124

Domaine Laroche is one of the most prestigious producers of chablis. Made from chardonnay, this delivers quality from start to finish. Look for lovely, elegant flavours that are focused and subtly layered, and a texture that's rich, refined and fresh. This is an excellent choice for shellfish, seafood, white fish and poultry.

NOTES
....
....
....
....

NEW!
★ ★ ★ ½

Dopf & Irion 'Crystal d'Alsace' Sylvaner 2010

AOC ALSACE $12.55   35667

Sylvaner used to be widely planted and used for making bulk wine. It's
less common now and is being treated more carefully, as this attractive
example shows. This is resolutely dry, with restrained and focused flavours
underpinned by vibrant, fresh acidity. It's a great choice for roast pork
and poultry, as well as for oysters, steamed mussels and other shellfish and
seafood.

NOTES

....

....

....

....

NEW!
★ ★ ★ ★

Dopf & Irion Gewürztraminer 2010

AOC ALSACE $16.05   81463

Gewürztraminer is one of the key grapes of Alsace, in eastern France,
which has become known as a region whose wines go well with Asian
food. This pungent, spicy, just off-dry wine has good intensity and the
right amount of acidity to complement and rein in the flavours without
interfering with their enjoyment. Try it yourself with Asian cuisine.

NOTES

....

....

....

....

....

★ ★ ★ ½

Fat Bastard Chardonnay 2010

VIN DE PAYS D'OC $14.95   663130

The flavours here are quite rich and intense, with a defined veneer of
oak—a style that many people like. The wine is medium weight and
dry, and the fruit is underpinned by a broad seam of fresh acidity, giving
the wine a refreshing texture that tilts it toward food. Pair this up with
poultry, pork and white fish.

NOTES

....

....

....

....

....

NEW!
★ ★ ★ ½

Jaffelin Bourgogne Aligoté 2010

AOC BOURGOGNE ALIGOTÉ $15.45   63868

Aligoté is a Burgundian grape variety that's perhaps best known as the wine used with cassis in making the aperitif kir. But it also makes worthy wine in its own right, as this example shows. It delivers attractive, fairly understated flavours, with a quite taut but balanced texture from the acidity. It makes a very good accompaniment to grilled white fish, trout and roasted chicken.

NOTES

....

....

....

....

NEW!
★ ★ ★ ★

Jaffelin Pouilly-Fuissé Chardonnay 2009

AOC POUILLY-FUISSÉ $24.95   242909

Pouilly-Fuissé is one of Burgundy's prestigious white wine appellations, and it's odd to see "chardonnay" on the label because it is the region that's the selling point. Still, this is a fine chardonnay, with well-calibrated and focused flavours underpinned by a seam of refreshing acidity. It goes very well with poached or grilled white fish, and roasted poultry and pork.

NOTES

....

....

....

....

★ ★ ★ ★ ½

La Chablisienne 'Les Vénérables' Vieilles Vignes Chablis 2008

AOC CHABLIS $24.95   942243

[Vintages Essential] There's no standard definition of "old vines" (*vieilles vignes*), but producers often use the term because older vines produce small quantities of higher-quality grapes. This is certainly a delicious and elegant chablis (made from chardonnay), with stylish and nuanced flavours, and a smooth, refreshing texture. Everything is in fine harmony and balance. Serve this with simple fish, chicken or pork dishes.

NOTES

....

....

....

....

NEW!
★ ★ ★ ★
La Vieille Ferme Luberon 2010

AOC LUBERON $11.95   298505

There are masses of little-known grape varieties in Mediterranean Europe—including ugni blanc and vermentino, which play a minor role to grenache blanc in this lovely white. There's nothing sophisticated here, just a well-made wine with complex, restrained flavours, great balance, and a smooth and crisp texture. It's perfect for sipping on its own and goes well with simple poultry, seafood and white fish dishes.

NOTES

....
....
....
....

NEW!
★ ★ ★ ★
Loron Bourgogne Chardonnay 2010

AOP BOURGOGNE $12.95   167155

Look for reasonable complexity in this attractive chardonnay. There are some sweet currents in the flavour profile, and the acidity is clean, crisp and well calibrated. This is dry and medium bodied, and it goes well with herbed roast chicken or pork, and white fish and seafood.

NOTES

....
....
....
....
....

NEW!
★ ★ ★ ½
Louis Bernard Côtes du Rhône 2010

AOC CÔTES DU RHÔNE $12.10   689565

Made from grenache blanc, bourboulenc and viognier, this dry, medium-bodied white blend delivers good quality across the board. The ripe flavours are consistent from start to finish, and they're very ably supported by a seam of acidity that makes the wine a palate-refreshing partner for food. Drink it with roasted poultry or pork, or with grilled white fish and seafood.

NOTES

....
....
....
....
....

★ ★ ★

Louis Jadot Bourgogne Chardonnay 2010

AOC BOURGOGNE $18.95   933077

[Vintages Essential] More and more French producers are adding the grape variety (chardonnay, in this case) to the region (Burgundy) on their labels to help consumers who buy wine by variety and not region. It makes no difference to the wine, which, in this case, has a very attractive and complex flavour profile, and a smooth yet crisp texture. It's medium bodied and dry, and goes well with grilled fish and seafood.

NOTES

....

....

....

....

NEW!
★ ★ ★

Louis Jadot Mâcon Villages Chardonnay 2010

AOC MÂCON VILLAGES $15.45   164145

Mâcon (pronounced mah-KON) is one of the many regions of Burgundy, and it is known for its chardonnay-based white wines. This one offers excellent fruit-acid balance, with nicely pitched and solid fruit on one side and refreshing, bright acidity on the other. It's medium bodied and dry, and makes a great partner for grilled white fish, poultry and pork as well as for many cream-based fish and meat dishes.

NOTES

....

....

....

....

★ ★ ★

Louis Latour Chardonnay 2010

AOC BOURGOGNE $16.45   65533

Nearly all white wines from Burgundy are made from chardonnay (just as the reds are made from pinot noir). They vary in style from lean and acidic to plump and fruity. This is a mid-range style, with concentrated and nuanced flavours, a round and smooth (but refreshing) texture, and very good balance. Drink it with chicken, turkey and soft mild cheeses like brie and camembert.

NOTES

....

....

....

....

NEW!
★★★ ½

Lurton Sauvignon 2010

AOC BORDEAUX $11.95   250381

Although New Zealand carried sauvignon blanc to its current popularity, the variety has been one of the major white grapes of Bordeaux for centuries. This example is in the more restrained style of bordeaux. The flavours are concentrated and well tuned, and they play well with the solid seam of crisp acidity. Dry and medium bodied, it goes very well with white fish and seafood, and with milder curries.

NOTES

....

....

....

....

★★★★

Mouton Cadet 2010

AOC BORDEAUX $13.45   2527

White bordeaux are too little known, as they tend to lie in the shadow of the famous reds. Take this white (or rather, buy it): a blend of semillon, sauvignon blanc and muscadelle. The flavours are bright and lively, and they flow consistently from start to finish. It's vibrant and refreshing— a white you can sip on its own or enjoy with seafood, steamed mussels, oysters or grilled white fish.

NOTES

....

....

....

....

NEW!
★★★★ ½

Mouton Cadet Réserve 2009

AOC GRAVES $14.95   247080

Graves is a small appellation in Bordeaux that is well known for its white wines. This blend of semillon, sauvignon blanc and muscadelle is attractive and stylish. The fruit is textured and nicely structured, with good complexity, and the acidity is clean and refreshing. It's dry and medium bodied, and makes an excellent wine for seafood, shellfish and white fish dishes.

NOTES

....

....

....

....

Pierre Sparr Gewürztraminer 2010

★ ★ ★ ★

AOC ALSACE $17.00   373373

Pierre Sparr is an Alsatian producer who does very well across his portfolio. This is a lovely, medium-bodied gewürztraminer with an opulent and plump texture that fills your mouth with flavour. As for that flavour, it's spicy, pungent and rich, with complexity to spare. If you're looking for a sparring partner for this wine, try a spicy Asian (especially Thai) dish.

NOTES

....

....

....

....

Pierre Sparr Riesling 2010

★ ★ ★ ★

AOC ALSACE $12.95   618546

This is a lovely riesling that's both delicate and substantial. It has a crisp and refreshing texture without any harshness, and the flavours are well extracted, nicely defined and yet understated. It's dry, medium bodied and very well balanced. If you're searching for a match, look no further than roasted chicken or pork, or grilled white fish or seafood.

NOTES

....

....

....

....

....

Rémy Pannier Anjou 2009

★ ★ ★ ½

AOC ANJOU $11.95   5967

Made from chenin blanc—which is probably the white grape variety most readily associated with the Loire Valley (where the Anjou appellation is located)—this delivers good, concentrated flavours that are both substantial and lively. The texture is quite round and smooth, but also refreshing, and this is a great choice for roasted poultry and pork. The fruitiness also extends it to spicy Asian cuisine.

NOTES

....

....

....

....

Sauvion 'Carte d'Or' Muscadet 2010

★ ★ ★ ★

AOC MUSCADET SÈVRE-ET-MAINE $12.95   143016

Muscadet, a Loire Valley region near the Atlantic coast, produces France's most popular wine to serve with fish. It can be bland and light, but this one has well-defined fruit flavours. It's medium bodied with an appealing and tangy texture, and it goes very well with all kinds of seafood. Try it with grilled white fish or with mussels steamed in white wine.

NOTES

....

....

....

....

....

William Fèvre 'Champs Royaux' Chablis 2010

★ ★ ★ ★ ½

AOC CHABLIS $21.55   276436

The classic wines from Chablis are chardonnays made and aged in stainless steel tanks, rather than in oak barrels. They offer pure and complex fruit flavours as this one does. It has a refreshing texture—not plush and mouth filling, but very crisp and clean. It's medium bodied and an excellent match for shellfish. Try it with mussels steamed in white wine and garlic.

NOTES

....

....

....

....

Willm Réserve Riesling 2010

NEW!
★ ★ ★ ★

AOC ALSACE $15.95   11452

[Vintages Essential] Alsatian riesling has a reputation all its own, and it's often a benchmark that New World rieslings are judged against. This one from Willm is quite luscious, with elegant flavours and the juicy, mouth-watering texture you expect from riesling. It's dry, fruity and medium bodied, and a great choice if you're eating shellfish or seafood. Or you can sip it on its own.

NOTES

....

....

....

....

GERMANY

WONDERFUL, GOOD-VALUE GERMAN WHITE WINES appear often in the LCBO's Vintages section, but the selection on the LCBO General Purchase list is often disappointing. Many people are put off German wines because they believe they're all sickly sweet. While it's true that many quality German wines do have some sweetness, it's not fake and cloying. It comes from the richness of the natural sugars in the grapes.

Important terms on German wine labels are *Prädikatswein* (the highest quality classification of wine) and *Qualitätswein* (sometimes followed by *b.A.*, and designates wines of quality but not of the highest level). *Landwein* indicates that the wine is made from grapes sourced from a broader region than the other classifications. Each of these terms is followed by the name of the wine region where the grapes were grown.

NEW!
★★★★ ½

Carl Reh Riesling Kabinett 2010

PRÄDIKATSWEIN MOSEL $12.95   174854

This is a delicious, off-dry riesling that we can only hope is part of the renewal of German wine offerings in the LCBO. It delivers plenty of ripe, defined flavours supported by a seam of bright, lively acidity. It's refreshing and you could easily sip this on its own, or pair it with well-seasoned or spicy poultry, pork and seafood dishes.

NOTES

NEW!
★★★ ½

Clean Slate Riesling 2010

QUALITÄTSWEIN B.A. MOSEL $12.95   286237

It's widely (and wrongly) believed that the soil and rock that vines grow in affect the flavour and texture of wine. Does this riesling taste of the slate that lies under the vineyards in the Mosel region? It's certainly clean, with good, crisp acidity cutting through the quite concentrated off-dry flavours. This is a good choice for rich foods, like foie gras, and also for many spicy foods, such as dishes inspired by Asian cuisine.

NOTES

GREECE

GREECE DOESN'T FEATURE PROMINENTLY on many people's wine radar (until they visit the country), but it produces a lot of wine that's good value. Although international grape varieties are becoming more popular there, it's good to see that many wines are still made using indigenous varieties.

Hatzimichalis Chardonnay 2010

REGIONAL WINE OF ATALANTI VALLEY $14.95   269654

Although most Greek wines are made from indigenous grape varieties, some—like this chardonnay—are made from international varieties. This is well made and attractive, with vibrant and nicely concentrated fruit flavours that are balanced by clean acidity. It goes well with grilled fish and chicken (serve them with lemon, as they would in Greece) and with mild, creamy cheeses.

NOTES

....

....

....

....

ITALY

ITALY HAS A LONG HISTORY of producing white wines from indigenous grapes, but in recent years we've seen more from international varieties, such as chardonnay. One international grape grown in many Italian regions is pinot grigio (also known as pinot gris). There are many mediocre pinot grigios, but this list identifies a number that stand out from the herd for quality and value.

The highest-quality classification of Italian wines is DOCG (*Denominazione di Origine Controllata e Garantita*), which indicates a wine made in accordance with stringent regulations and from a few specified grape varieties. Wines in the next category, DOC (*Denominazione di Origine Controllata*), follow similar but somewhat less rigorous rules. Wines labelled IGT (*Indicazione Geografica Tipica*) or IGP (*Indicazione Geografica Protetta*) are made according to even less-stringent regulations and may use a wider range of grape varieties. This doesn't mean that a DOCG wine is necessarily better than an IGT/IGP. In fact, some of Italy's most famous wines are IGT/IGP wines. Overall, you'll find quality and value in all these categories, as this list shows.

NEW!
★★★★

Anselmi San Vincenzo 2010

IGT VENETO $14.95 948158

[Vintages Essential] From northeastern Italy, this is a blend of an Italian grape, garganega, and two international varieties, chardonnay and sauvignon blanc. It's a ménage à trois that works. Look for sweet fruit in this dry wine, finely balanced by bright, crisp acidity. It's a great wine for summer sipping or as an aperitif, and it goes well with many seafood, fish and poultry dishes.

NOTES

....

....

....

....

NEW!
★★★★ ½

Cavallina Grillo/Pinot Grigio 2010

IGT SICILIA $7.55 123166

Grillo is a grape variety widely planted in Sicily because it can withstand the high temperatures. It produces high acidity that translates as a zesty, vibrant texture, the sort you see here. Blended with pinot grigio for fruit flavour, it makes an easy-drinking white on its own. It also pairs well with spicy dishes and many ways of preparing chicken, white fish, shellfish and seafood.

NOTES

....

....

....

....

★★★ ½

Citra Trebbiano d'Abruzzo 2010

DOC TREBBIANO D'ABRUZZO $6.95 622144

Like many Italian wine names, this one combines a grape variety (trebbiano) and a region (Abruzzo). The wine is medium bodied and has an attractively dry feel. Look for very pleasant and fairly complex fruit flavours here, and a clean and refreshing texture that makes for a good match with creamy Italian dishes. Try it with fettuccine alfredo or any pasta prepared in a cream sauce.

NOTES

....

....

....

....

Collavini 'Villa Canlungo' Pinot Grigio 2010

★ ★ ★ ½

IGT VENEZIA GULIA $14.95 33340

This is a dry, medium-bodied pinot grigio. Its very good balance strikes you first. There's a vibrant and tangy texture here that makes this a versatile food wine, as good with roast chicken as with seafood and fish, or even slightly spicy dishes. The flavours are concentrated and ripe, and they show decent complexity.

NOTES

....

....

....

....

....

NEW!
★ ★ ★ ★

Danzante Pinot Grigio 2010

IGT DELLE VENEZIE $13.45 26906

"Dance the pure emotion of Italian wine," the label urges. Well, the texture in this pinot grigio is lively and refreshing, and it's in step with the flavours, which are nicely paced, decently complex and concentrated. Neither leads—they dance side by side. If you want to add another partner (this could get complicated), try grilled white fish, herbed roast chicken or grilled garlic shrimp.

NOTES

....

....

....

....

★ ★ ★ ★

Fazi Battaglia Verdicchio dei Castelli di Jesi Classico 2010

DOC VERDICCHIO DEI CASTELLI DI JESI CLASSICO

$9.95 24422

Fazi Battaglia packages its verdicchio in a distinctive bottle that looks a bit like an elongated Coca-Cola bottle. But the contents are much, much better. There are lovely fruit flavours, and a touch of tanginess for good measure. With its fine balance and crisp texture, this wine is ideal for drinking alongside many kinds of seafood and white fish.

NOTES

....

....

....

....

NEW!
★★★ ½

Folonari Pinot Grigio 2010

IGT DELLE VENEZIE $13.95   229542

Sometimes it seems the Italian section at the LCBO is nothing but pinot grigio. It's not so, of course, but there are a lot of them, and it's nice to pick out the better examples. This is one. It shows solid and attractive fruit and a good seam of fresh acidity that makes you want another sip. It goes well with cream-based pasta, poultry and pork. And, of course, you can sip it on its own.

NOTES
....
....
....
....

★★★★ ½

Gabbiano Pinot Grigio 2010

IGT TOSCANA $12.95   77990

The Castello di Gabbiano, home of this winery, is a thirteenth-century castle in Tuscany that is now also an elegant hotel. This pinot grigio is equally elegant. It shows lovely flavours that are fresh and substantial, and a texture that's round, smooth and very refreshing. Dry and medium bodied, this is a wine you can sip as an aperitif or drink with rich or slightly spicy seafood, chicken, turkey or pork.

NOTES
....
....
....
....

★★★★

Lamberti 'Santepietre' Pinot Grigio 2010

IGT DELLE VENEZIE $12.95   660524

This is a pinot grigio in a style that's leaner and crisper than many others, and it makes a great partner for food. The flavours are nicely concentrated and have some complexity, and the texture is clean, vibrant and brisk. It's dry and medium bodied, and a very good choice when you're having grilled white fish, shellfish (such as steamed mussels in white wine and garlic) or a simple chicken dish.

NOTES
....
....
....
....

Masi Masianco 2010

NEW!
★ ★ ★ ★ ½

IGT VENEZIE $13.95 620773

This is a very attractive blend of pinot grigio and verduzzo, with the verduzzo having been dried before being pressed in order to increase intensity and complexity. The result is a white with real depth, plus fresh fruitiness from the pinot grigio. Dry and medium weight, it's refreshing on its own and excellent paired with poultry, white fish, seafood and pork.

NOTES

....

....

....

....

....

Montalto Pinot Grigio 2011

★ ★ ★ ★

IGT SICILIA $8.95 73148

This is a sibling to rival Montalto Nero d'Avola/Cabernet Sauvignon (see page 174), and it's a reminder that Sicily used to be predominantly a white wine producer. This dry pinot grigio has lovely rich flavours that are nicely nuanced, and a tangy, fresh texture. It's an ideal partner for white fish and seafood, and it will also suit not-too-spicy sushi.

NOTES

....

....

....

....

Placido Pinot Grigio 2011

NEW!
★ ★ ★ ★ ½

IGT DELLE VENEZIE $12.10 688897

From northeastern Italy, this pinot grigio really stands out from many others. Drunk chilled, not too cold, it's almost elegant in style, with well-defined and focused flavours, good complexity and a finely integrated line of acidity that's both refreshing and soft. Dry and medium bodied, this is a great choice for many dishes, such as chicken, pork, fish and creamy pasta.

NOTES

....

....

....

....

NEW!
★ ★ ★ ★ ½

Santa Margherita Pinot Grigio 2010

DOC VALDADIGE $16.95 106450

[Vintages Essential] This is a popular pinot grigio and the secret of its success is its balance. Everything here harmonizes beautifully. It has enough of everything, but not too much of anything. The acidity and fruit complement each other well, and the flavours are neither too forward nor too restrained. It makes an excellent sipping wine before a meal, but also teams beautifully with food, especially seafood.

NOTES
....
....
....
....

NEW!
★ ★ ★ ★

Zenato Soave Classico

DOC SOAVE $12.75 268417

Made in the Soave region in Veneto, this delivers solid and attractive flavours that are sweet in the centre and paired with brisk, crisp acidity. It's dry and medium bodied, and it goes well with roast chicken or pork.

NOTES
....
....
....
....
....
....

NEW ZEALAND

NEW ZEALAND IS A VERY SMALL PRODUCER of wine in global terms, but it made a big name for itself in the wine world in the 1990s with sauvignon blancs, especially those from Marlborough. They're still the core of the country's white wines, but chardonnay and other white varieties (and other regions) are definitely worth trying.

Alpine Valley Sauvignon Blanc 2011

NEW!
★★★★

MARLBOROUGH $14.95   241810

The Marlborough wine region, which is New Zealand's biggest, lies in the north of the South Island, at the northern end of the Southern Alps— a snow-capped range that runs all the way to the Central Otago wine region. This "savvy" (as it's called in NZ) is bright and fresh, with quite dense and pungent flavours, and a juicy texture. It's a good choice for oysters, seafood and white fish.

NOTES

....
....
....
....

Babich Sauvignon Blanc 2010

★★★★ ½

MARLBOROUGH $14.95   620054

The Babich family first cultivated vines early in the twentieth century near Auckland, but the grapes for this wine come from much farther south— the famed Marlborough region. It gives the wine its classic New Zealand sauvignon flavours of exciting and pungent fruit. It's crisp and refreshing, with a smooth texture, and it goes wonderfully with warm goat cheese salad or tomato and goat cheese quiche.

NOTES

....
....
....
....

Brancott Sauvignon Blanc 2011

NEW!
★★★★

MARLBOROUGH $11.95   129528

Here's another luscious, but less expensive, sauvignon blanc from Marlborough, offering that great one-two combination of rich, ripe, complex fruit flavours and a burst of refreshing tanginess that makes you whimper for a plate of oysters or white fish irrigated with lemon juice. Some of these sauvignons are a bit over the top in flavour and acidity, but this one keeps everything in the right place.

NOTES

....
....
....
....

Kim Crawford Sauvignon Blanc 2011

★ ★ ★ ★ ½

MARLBOROUGH $18.95   35386

[Vintages Essential] Kim Crawford is an iconic New Zealand winemaker, one of the pioneers of the new wine industry in the country. And this is just about an iconic wine, too, with classic New Zealand sauvignon blanc characteristics. The flavours are rich, layered and pungent, and the mouthfeel is plush and zesty. This is a fine wine to drink with grilled herbed white fish and fresh lemon.

NOTES

Matua Valley Sauvignon Blanc 2011

★ ★ ★ ★ ½

HAWKES BAY $15.95   619452

If you're feeling a little jaded from your diet of Marlborough sauvignon blanc, try this one from Hawkes Bay, a region on New Zealand's North Island. It's a little different, a little fruitier, but it has the same style of plush and well-focused fruit flavours, together with a full and refreshing texture. This is a great choice if you're having grilled white fish or seafood, but try it with mussels steamed in white wine and garlic, too.

NOTES

Mud House Sauvignon Blanc 2010

NEW!
★ ★ ★ ★

MARLBOROUGH $15.95   190454

This is a very well-made sauvignon blanc from New Zealand's key sauvignon region. The flavours are attractive, concentrated and consistent from front to back, and the broad seam of fresh acidity gives it a *salivant* (or mouth-watering) quality that sets you up for food. Serve this with oysters, seafood, white fish or mild-to-medium hot curries.

NOTES

★ ★ ★ ★

Oyster Bay Sauvignon Blanc 2011

MARLBOROUGH $16.95   316570

[Vintages Essential] Here's a well-named wine. One of the classic food pairings with sauvignon blanc is freshly shucked oysters. The richness and acidity of the wine pick up the texture and brininess of the shellfish. This sauv blanc is quite lovely, with concentrated and pungent flavours that flow in on a tide that's crisp and refreshing. If you don't have fresh oysters to hand, try grilled white fish with fresh lemon.

NOTES

....

....

....

....

NEW!
★ ★ ★ ★

The People's Pinot Gris 2010

HAWKES BAY $16.95   240978

Drawing on grapes from the Hawkes Bay wine region, on the east coast of the North Island, this attractive, dry pinot gris goes well with well-seasoned or spicy dishes featuring seafood, white fish, chicken and pork. It has a smooth, quite plush texture, fruit that's sweet and solid from start to finish, and very good fruit-acid balance.

NOTES

....

....

....

....

....

★ ★ ★ ★

Stoneleigh Chardonnay 2010

MARLBOROUGH $16.95   288795

From New Zealand's famous Marlborough region (best known for its sauvignon blancs) comes this delicious chardonnay. It's packed with ripe, fresh, vibrant fruit flavours that are concentrated and nuanced. They're accompanied by a rich, plush, refreshing texture that makes you think of food. It's dry and excellently balanced, and goes very well with chicken, turkey or pork.

NOTES

....

....

....

....

Stoneleigh Sauvignon Blanc 2011

★ ★ ★ ★

MARLBOROUGH $16.95   293043

Marlborough gets more sunshine each year than almost any other part of New Zealand. Combine that with cool temperatures, and you have perfect conditions for sauvignon blancs like this one. The fruit is ripe, sweet and pungent, and it's undergirded with vibrant acidity. The result is a mouth-watering wine that's an ideal dinner accompaniment. Seafood, shellfish and white fish are the classics, but try it with curried dishes, too.

NOTES

....

....

....

....

Villa Maria 'Private Bin' Sauvignon Blanc 2011

★ ★ ★ ★

MARLBOROUGH $15.95   426601

Villa Maria is a well-established New Zealand winery that I used to visit when I was a teenager living in Auckland. It has since been transformed from a small local producer to a global exporter, thanks to wines like this sauvignon blanc. It delivers concentrated and nicely defined flavours, and a rich and zesty texture that picks up the natural acidity of the grape variety. It's an ideal choice for grilled white fish with a squeeze of lemon.

NOTES

....

....

....

....

Whitecliff Sauvignon Blanc 2010

★ ★ ★ ★

MARLBOROUGH $14.95   610972

This is a sauvignon blanc made in the classic Marlborough style that first put New Zealand on the wine map. The flavours are rich, pungent, complex and well defined, and there's a terrific seam of acidity running right through it, contributing a clean, bright and zesty texture. It's a real palate cleanser and goes well with oysters or perhaps a tomato and goat cheese tart.

NOTES

....

....

....

....

ONTARIO

SOME OF THE BEST WINES produced in Ontario are white. The cool growing conditions allow the grapes to ripen while achieving the levels of acidity they need to be crisp and refreshing. The most successful white varieties in the province are riesling, chardonnay, sauvignon blanc and gewürztraminer.

The initials VQA (Vintners Quality Alliance) on an Ontario wine label, followed by the name of a wine region, mean that the wine was made from grapes grown in that region and has been tested and tasted for quality. Wines labelled VQA with an Ontario region can be made only from grapes grown in Ontario. The designated wine regions are Niagara Peninsula (and its sub-regions, such as Beamsville Bench and Niagara-on-the-Lake), Lake Erie North Shore, Pelee Island and Prince Edward County.

Non-VQA wines in the LCBO's Canada and Ontario sections are usually blends of a small percentage of Ontario wine and a high percentage of foreign wine. They are not included in this book.

NEW!
★★★★
Cave Spring Chardonnay 2010
VQA NIAGARA ESCARPMENT $14.95   228551

Wine writers occasionally refer to the ABC movement, meaning
Anything But Chardonnay, because, supposedly, many people are tired
of chardonnay. This might change their minds. For the price, it's quite
rich and stylish, with solid, mouth-filling fruit flavours, and it has a
fresh and juicy texture. You'll enjoy this with lobster, or with rich turkey,
chicken and pork dishes.

NOTES
....
....
....
....

★★★★
Cave Spring Dry Riesling 2010
VQA NIAGARA PENINSULA $14.95   233635

Cave Spring quickly established a reputation for riesling, and it's still
among the best producers in Ontario. Its rieslings tend to be stylish and
complex, and they go beautifully with food. This one has a crisp and yet
generous texture that's complemented by lovely nuanced fruit flavours. It's
dry, refreshing and medium bodied. You can sip it as an aperitif, but it has
the stuff to go with smoked chicken or pork tenderloin.

NOTES
....
....
....
....

★★★★ ½
Cave Spring 'Estate Bottled' Riesling 2010
VQA BEAMSVILLE BENCH $17.95   286377

[Vintages Essential] Beamsville Bench is one of more than a dozen sub-
appellations (or sub-regions) that the Niagara Peninsula appellation (wine
region) has been divided into. It might be a bit confusing for consumers,
but what's not confusing is this only-just-off-dry riesling. It delivers
delicious, intense flavours on a texture that's brisk and clean and makes
you want to eat. So eat. Drink this with spicy seafood or smoked salmon.

NOTES
....
....
....
....

Cave Spring Riesling 2010

★ ★ ★ ★ ½   VQA NIAGARA PENINSULA $14.95   234583

Cave Spring winemaker Angelo Pavan hasn't lost his magic touch with riesling. This is a gorgeous off-dry example that displays rich, luscious, well-nuanced fruit flavours, accompanied by a texture that's plush and mouth filling, but also zesty and refreshing. It's the perfect wine for slightly spicy seafood, chicken and pork dishes, or for Thai or Indian food, whether vegetarian or meat-based.

NOTES

....
....
....
....
....

Cave Spring Sauvignon Blanc 2010

★ ★ ★ ★   VQA NIAGARA PENINSULA $15.95   629933

This is a lovely sauvignon blanc that goes well with grilled white fish with a squeeze of lemon, freshly shucked oysters or fish and chips (but avoid vinegar and stick to lemon). Made in a classic and popular style, this sauvignon is dry and medium bodied, with a refreshing and zesty texture that lifts and enhances the well-defined and quite concentrated flavours.

NOTES

....
....
....
....

Château des Charmes Aligoté 2010

★ ★ ★ ★   VQA ST. DAVID'S BENCH $13.55   284950

Aligoté is a little-known variety from Burgundy, where most of the white wine is made from chardonnay. This example has the crisp texture and clean, refreshing aftertaste that's characteristic of the variety, making it ideal for shellfish. It has rich and concentrated flavours, and a fairly round mouthfeel. Try it with roasted chicken or grilled pork chops, too.

NOTES

....
....
....
....
....

★ ★ ★ ★ ½

Château des Charmes 'Barrel Fermented' Chardonnay 2010

VQA NIAGARA-ON-THE-LAKE $13.95   81653

This is an especially delicious chardonnay in a style that I find irresistible because it seamlessly combines weight and elegance. Look for plush and well-defined fruit that's nicely complex, and a round, smooth, mouth-filling, refreshing texture. It shows terrific balance, and is an excellent choice for poultry and pork, and even rich dishes like lobster and seared scallops.

NOTES

....

....

....

....

★ ★ ★ ★

Château des Charmes Riesling 2009

VQA NIAGARA-ON-THE-LAKE $12.55   61499

Niagara-on-the-Lake is one of several smaller wine regions (sub-appellations) within the larger Niagara Peninsula region that can now be shown on wine labels, as long as all the grapes in the wine were grown there. These riesling grapes have produced a very attractive, medium-bodied and essentially dry wine with a smooth, crisp texture and focused fruity flavours. Drink it with roast chicken, pork or seafood.

NOTES

....

....

....

★ ★ ★ ★

Château des Charmes Sauvignon Blanc 2010

VQA ST. DAVID'S BENCH $14.95   391300

St. David's Bench is a sub-appellation (wine sub-region) within the Niagara Peninsula wine region. This sauvignon blanc is really lovely, with lively and bright (but also solid and substantial) flavours, and a texture that's refreshing and vibrant. It's dry and medium bodied, and an excellent wine to serve with grilled white fish and freshly squeezed lemon (or with fish and chips—but hold the vinegar).

NOTES

....

....

....

....

Coyote's Run Five Mile White 2010

NEW!
★ ★ ★ ★

VQA NIAGARA PENINSULA $14.25 195669

This is a blend of riesling, pinot blanc and chardonnay, all varieties that do well in Ontario. It's slightly off-dry (off-dry-dry?), with bright and somewhat pungent flavours allied with a broad seam of vibrant acidity. It's the style of wine that's frequently suggested for spicy food, and this one goes well with sushi and Thai cuisine.

NOTES

Creekside Pinot Grigio 2010

★ ★ ★ ★

VQA NIAGARA PENINSULA $14.95 83196

This is a quite luscious pinot grigio with well-defined and complex flavours and a great clean, crisp, refreshing texture. There's a pink tinge to the wine from the grape skins, which are often a brownish-pink colour. It's not as fruity as many pinot grigios, and the texture makes it an excellent choice for many foods. Try it with chicken, pork and shellfish (like mussels steamed in white wine).

NOTES

Fielding Estate Pinot Gris 2010

NEW!
★ ★ ★ ★

VQA NIAGARA PENINSULA $18.95 223610

There's a little sweetness here, but don't avoid this if your preference is for dry wines. The flavour complexity and the well-calibrated acidity give the wine a dry feel, and it ends quite astringently. Medium bodied and quite elegant, this is a great choice for spicy seafood, shellfish or poultry dishes, whether or not they're Asian-inspired.

NOTES

Fielding Estate Riesling 2009

★ ★ ★ ★

VQA NIAGARA PENINSULA　　　　　$15.75　　　　146761

Fielding's logo is a Muskoka chair, and this is the kind of wine you want when you kick back to relax. It's off-dry with plenty of acidity to smooth things out and give you a crisp, clean feel in your mouth. Sip it on its own, serve it as an aperitif or drink it with spicy Asian dishes or melon and prosciutto.

NOTES

....

....

....

....

....

NEW!
★ ★ ★ ★
Fielding Estate White Conception 2010

VQA NIAGARA PENINSULA　　　　　$18.95　　　　203737

An interesting blend of chardonnay, sauvignon blanc, viognier and gewürzrtraminer, this wine shows substance, complexity and vibrancy. The tension is evident in both the flavour—which is complex and sweet-centred—and the full but clean and crisp texture. The viognier/gewürz pushes toward spicy dishes, the chard and sauvignon toward roasted chicken and grilled fish. They all work. You decide.

NOTES

....

....

....

....

NEW!
★ ★ ★ ★ ½
Flat Rock Twisted 2010

VQA TWENTY MILE BENCH　　　　　$16.95　　　　1578

[Vintages Essential] "Twisted" is a blend of gewürztraminer, riesling and chardonnay. Putting those three varieties together might have seemed like a twisted notion at first, but it worked. This wine is full of rich, focused and pungent ripe fruit, backed up by a good dose of zesty acidity. It's intense and juicy, and forms a great partnership with spicy dishes.

NOTES

....

....

....

....

....

NEW!
★★★ ½

Generation Seven White 2010

VQA NIAGARA-ON-THE-LAKE $13.95   197988

Made from riesling, sauvignon blanc and gewürztraminer, this is one of
several Ontario wines made in an easy-drinking style for the mass market.
They don't all work, but this one does. Look for solid flavours of pungent,
sweet fruit harnessed to bright, zesty acidity. It's not complicated or
complex, but it goes very well with spicy Asian cuisine and many poultry
and pork dishes. Or drink it just by itself.

NOTES

....
....
....
....

★★★★

Henry of Pelham Chardonnay 2010

VQA NIAGARA PENINSULA $13.95   291211

This wine was made and aged in stainless steel to preserve the purity of
the fruit flavours. It worked. This is just a very well-made wine—nothing
to make you run screaming into the street, but a wine to enjoy. The sweet
and ripe flavours are substantial but nuanced and delicate, and the texture
is clean and refreshing. It's a natural for roast chicken or pork and for
simple white fish dishes.

NOTES

....
....
....
....

★★★★

Henry of Pelham Riesling 2010

VQA NIAGARA PENINSULA $13.95   268375

Riesling has led the way with screw caps—first in New Zealand and
Australia, and then elsewhere. The seal captures the freshness you want in
the variety, and Henry of Pelham delivers. This dry riesling is packed with
delicious flavour, together with a mouth-filling and zesty texture. It's a
good choice for sipping on the deck or before dinner, and it's also excellent
with fish, seafood, chicken or pork dishes.

NOTES

....
....
....
....

Henry of Pelham Sauvignon Blanc 2011

★ ★ ★ ★

VQA NIAGARA PENINSULA $14.95 430546

Although the label doesn't show it, this is a single-vineyard wine. It's a very attractive sauvignon blanc, and it has all the crispness of texture and brightness of fruit you look for in this variety, without the pungency that often overpowers food. The flavours are lively and textured, it's dry and medium bodied, and it goes well with shellfish, seafood and grilled or pan-fried white fish with fresh lemon.

NOTES
....
....
....
....

Inniskillin Oak-Aged Chardonnay 2009

NEW!
★ ★ ★ ★

VQA NIAGARA PENINSULA $14.95 317768

If you've ever wondered what difference oak-aging makes to wine, try this and the following chardonnay. The difference might not be wholly due to the aging, but it gives you an idea of the influence that the oak has. This is quite plush and full in texture, with ripe, sweet fruit flavours and very good fruit-acid balance. Drink it with herbed roast chicken, grilled salmon and white fish, or roasted pork.

NOTES
....
....
....
....

Inniskillin Unoaked Chardonnay 2009

NEW!
★ ★ ★ ½

VQA NIAGARA PENINSULA $12.95 66266

Inniskillin winery was named for Inniskillin Farm, which, after the War of 1812, was a land grant to a colonel in the Inniskillin Fusiliers. This is an uncomplicated chardonnay with well-defined flavours. It's dry with medium body and a solid and very refreshing texture—the sort of wine you can sip on its own in the afternoon or enjoy with roasted or grilled chicken, white fish and seafood, or cream-based pasta dishes.

NOTES
....
....
....
....

NEW!
★ ★ ★ ★

Jackson-Triggs 'Black Series' Gewürztraminer 2010

VQA NIAGARA PENINSULA $12.95   626269

This gewürztraminer is made in a very attractive style—not too blowsy, but with flavours that are nicely tuned and have a certain delicacy, while the texture is both mouth filling and spicy. There's a hint of the clean bitterness that you often get with this variety, which I like. Drink it with spicy seafood or with Thai dishes.

NOTES

....

....

....

....

....

NEW!
★ ★ ★ ★ ½

Jackson-Triggs Reserve Riesling 2011

VQA NIAGARA PENINSULA $11.45   626277

This is a lovely riesling just bursting with rich, ripe fruit. There's good concentration and complexity, and the fruit is supported by vibrant acidity that lends the wine a juicy texture. It's off-dry, with the acidity off-setting the sugar nicely. This is a great choice for spicy dishes, but it's refreshing enough that you can enjoy it on its own, too.

NOTES

....

....

....

....

....

NEW!
★ ★ ★ ★ ½

Kacaba Unoaked Chardonnay 2009

VQA NIAGARA ESCARPMENT $14.95   101469

If you think chardonnay needs a touch of oak to give it character, try this. It's a really lovely wine with a smooth, full texture, and flavours that are restrained yet concentrated and defined and that span a good spectrum of notes. Dry and medium bodied, it has notable fruit purity, and it's an excellent partner for roasted poultry and pork, as well as grilled white fish.

NOTES

....

....

....

....

Konzelmann Pinot Blanc 2010

★ ★ ★ ½

VQA NIAGARA PENINSULA $12.15 219279

Konzelmann Estate Winery is located near Niagara-on-the-Lake, close to the shore of Lake Ontario. This pinot blanc (*weissburgunder*, the grape's name in German, is included on the label) delivers attractive and quite intense fruity flavours, with a round, smooth but refreshing texture. This is a good sipping wine, and it will also go well with chicken and pork tenderloin.

NOTES

....

....

....

....

Malivoire Chardonnay 2010

★ ★ ★ ★

VQA NIAGARA PENINSULA $19.95 673147

[Vintages Essential] Malivoire was one of the first wineries to use a gravity-fed system in which the wine flows naturally from crush to barrels without any pumping. This lovely chardonnay shows attractive fruit flavours that are layered and complex, complemented by a juicy texture that's satisfying and refreshing. Dry and medium bodied, it's a very good partner for roast poultry or pork.

NOTES

....

....

....

....

Malivoire 'Guilty Men' White 2010

NEW!
★ ★ ★ ★

VQA NIAGARA PENINSULA $14.95 192666

It's not clear what these men are guilty of, but the 666 in the LCBO number suggests it's something diabolical. Yet . . . the blend of riesling, sauvignon blanc and chardonnay not only sounds innocent enough, it's very attractive and compelling. The fruit is focused and complex, the acidity is lively and refreshing, and it's a great choice for drinking on its own or with spicy, perhaps Asian, dishes.

NOTES

....

....

....

....

Megalomaniac 'Homegrown Cellar 4379' Riesling 2011

NEW!
★★★★

VQA NIAGARA PENINSULA $12.95   183061

The label tells the story behind the name, so read it as you open the bottle to pour with spicy seafood, chicken, tofu or vegetarian dishes—maybe with takeout Thai. The wine shows pure fruit that's nicely complex, complemented by clean, zesty acidity. It's in an off-dry style, with great balance among the components.

NOTES

....

....

....

....

....

Mike Weir Chardonnay 2008

★★★ ½

VQA NIAGARA PENINSULA $14.95   26

[Vintages Essential] Yes, that is product code number 26, not Mike's score around nine holes. The chardonnay plays well right through the course. It drives off with quite intense and decently complex flavours, and hits the fairway with a taut texture offset by good acidity. It's as dry as a summer day on the links, and medium bodied. You'll be popular putting this out (get it?) when you're serving roasted chicken or grilled salmon.

NOTES

....

....

....

....

Peller Estates 'Family Series' Riesling 2010

NEW!
★★★ ½

VQA NIAGARA PENINSULA $11.95   682817

This is a very approachable riesling in a style that will appeal to people who are put off by the more acidic versions and who also want a dry white. That said, it retains all the character of the variety, with a pleasantly crisp texture and very attractive flavours that run right through the palate. Drink it with roast chicken or pork.

NOTES

....

....

....

....

Peninsula Ridge 'Inox' Chardonnay 2009

★ ★ ★ ★ ½

VQA NIAGARA PENINSULA $13.95   694200

This chardonnay spends no time at all in oak barrels. 'Inox' refers to the stainless steel tanks that the wine is made in, which present the fruit flavours and texture without any oak influence. What you get here are beautifully clean, pure flavours and just excellent balance. It's almost full bodied, with a generous texture, and excellent with pork, chicken and white fish.

NOTES

....

....

....

....

Peninsula Ridge Sauvignon Blanc 2010

★ ★ ★ ★ ½

VQA NIAGARA PENINSULA $13.95   63678

Peninsula Ridge was the first winery where I tasted an Ontario sauvignon blanc that I thought was stunning. It's vintage variable, but this one is full of sauvignon character, with clean and pungent fruit flavours, a fairly full texture that's quite high in refreshing acidity, and a long, clean finish. Drink it with the usual suspects—freshly shucked oysters—or with battered white fish, chips and tartar sauce.

NOTES

....

....

....

....

Pillitteri 'Fusion' Gewürztraminer/Riesling 2010

NEW!
★ ★ ★ ★

VQA NIAGARA-ON-THE-LAKE $12.95   349126

This is a luscious, medium-bodied blend that brings together . . . er, fuses . . . the rich flavours and texture of gewürztraminer and the raciness of riesling, and it's very successful. You get intensely pungent and sweet fruit flavours lifted by a texture that's both plush and refreshing. This goes well with spicy food, so think of it for Asian dishes with pork, chicken, seafood or tofu.

NOTES

....

....

....

....

NEW!
★ ★ ★ ★
Pillitteri Pinot Grigio 2010
VQA NIAGARA-ON-THE-LAKE $12.95   146787

There was a time, a few years ago, when pinot grigio was slated to be the chardonnay-slayer and become the world's most popular white. It didn't happen, but you can see why many people rallied to pinot grigio. This one has concentrated, fresh flavours, and a vibrant and refreshing texture. Dry and medium bodied, it goes well with white fish, shellfish, poultry and pork, and has the fruitiness to handle many spicy dishes.

NOTES

....

....

....

....

NEW!
★ ★ ★ ½
Sibling Rivalry White 2010
VQA NIAGARA PENINSULA $13.95   126144

A blend of riesling, chardonnay and gewürztraminer, this is made by Henry of Pelham. The company is owned by three brothers—which might just explain the name of the brand. The wine itself is quite harmonious, however: a fruity white with enough complexity and good fruit-acid balance. Drink it on its own or with spicy chicken or seafood dishes.

NOTES

....

....

....

....

....

NEW!
★ ★ ★ ★
Southbrook 'Connect' White 2011
VQA ONTARIO $14.95   249078

This is 100 percent vidal, a hybrid variety sometimes used for icewine, often for blending, but rarely for a quality wine in its own right. This is one of the exceptions. It's a very attractive—and organic—white that has plenty of fruit and good intensity, and a bright and crisp texture. It's easy-drinking on its own and a very good option for sushi and other spicy Asian dishes.

NOTES

....

....

....

....

NEW!
★ ★ ★ ★ ½

Stoney Ridge Unoaked Chardonnay 2010

VQA TWENTY MILE BENCH $12.95 146795

Twenty Mile Bench is one of the sub-appellations of the Niagara Peninsula. The chardonnay, made only from grapes grown in the sub-appellation, shows lovely pure fruit that's understated and defined, complemented by clean, fresh acidity. It's dry and medium bodied, and quite elegant, and it goes very well with roasted poultry or grilled white fish and seafood.

NOTES

....

....

....

....

NEW!
★ ★ ★ ½

Strewn Dry Gewürztraminer 2009

VQA NIAGARA PENINSULA $12.95 65359

Gewürztraminer is an underappreciated variety (maybe because it looks difficult to pronounce), which is a pity, because it does well in Niagara. This might not be a stellar example, but it shows good, understated flavours with concentration and modest complexity, with fresh acidity and the telltale (and attractive) hint of bitterness at the end. Drink it with roast chicken or pork.

NOTES

....

....

....

....

NEW!
★ ★ ★ ½

Strewn 'Two Vines' Riesling/Gewürztraminer 2010

VQA ONTARIO $11.95 467662

The name of this winery has no relation to wine, location or the owners' names. They were simply looking for a word that was pithy and neutral, and "strewn" fitted the bill. This off-dry blend combines the rich flavours of gewürztraminer and the zestiness of riesling. It makes a great aperitif to whet your appetite, or to partner spicy—possibly Asian-inspired—dishes of seafood, chicken or pork.

NOTES

....

....

....

....

Thirty Bench Riesling 2010

NEW!
★ ★ ★ ★ ½

VQA BEAMSVILLE BENCH $18.95   24133

Thirty Bench is a winery with a deserved reputation for making fine
rieslings, and this one fits the portfolio well. The flavours are rich, ripe
and pungent, with very good, layered complexity. They're underpinned
by a broad seam of lively acidity that comes through as juiciness, a texture
that invites food. This is a great choice for well-seasoned or spicy seafood,
poultry or pork, and for many Asian dishes.

NOTES

....

....

....

....

Top Bench White 2010

NEW!
★ ★ ★ ½

VQA NIAGARA PENINSULA $13.95   226803

Made by Peninsula Ridge, this is one of the more successful of the brands
produced by Niagara Peninsula wineries to appeal to a wider range of
consumers. Top Bench White starts quite aromatically, but the style
is dry and even somewhat austere. The flavours are fairly concentrated
and interesting, the fruit-acid balance is good, and it's a good choice for
poultry, pork and seafood.

NOTES

....

....

....

....

Trius Chardonnay 2010

★ ★ ★ ★

VQA NIAGARA PENINSULA $13.95   497248

This chardonnay exhibits lovely, rich fruit flavours. They're concentrated
and nicely structured, and the fruit/acid balance is excellent. It's a
compelling combination that's intense, yet surprisingly light on its feet.
Dry, medium bodied and with a smooth, crisp texture, it's a great choice
for chicken, fish and seafood, and has the weight to handle roasted and
grilled pork, too.

NOTES

....

....

....

....

Trius Riesling Dry 2010

★ ★ ★ ★

VQA NIAGARA PENINSULA $13.95 303792

With so many good-quality and good-value rieslings around—like this one—it's a pity that the variety isn't more popular. Maybe it's because many people still associate it with older-style sweet wines. Ontario produces many fabulous rieslings. This one is just slightly off-dry, full of lovely, vibrant fruit flavours, and has a lively, crisp texture. It's medium bodied, and an excellent choice for rich seafood, chicken or pork dishes.

NOTES

....
....
....
....

NEW!
★ ★ ★ ★ Trius Sauvignon Blanc 2011

VQA NIAGARA PENINSULA $13.95 221804

Looking for a sauvignon blanc, yet wanting a change from New Zealand? Try this very good "savvy" (as it's known in New Zealand) in the reliable Trius line. The flavours are pungent yet bright, and the seam of vibrant acidity makes for a fresh and juicy texture. It goes very well with the usual suspects—oysters, seafood, white fish—and also with many poultry dishes and mild curries.

NOTES

....
....
....
....

NEW!
★ ★ ★ ★ Trumpour's Mill Pinot Gris 2010

VQA PRINCE EDWARD COUNTY $14.95 69336

Made by the Grange of Prince Edward winery, this pinot gris starts aromatically, then shifts gear to fairly taut and understated flavours that deliver good complexity and breadth. The acidity shows through as vibrant freshness, and this dry white makes an excellent and versatile addition to your table. Serve it with poultry, white fish and pork.

NOTES

....
....
....
....
....

NEW!
★ ★ ★ ★

Trumpour's Mill Riesling 2009

VQA PRINCE EDWARD COUNTY $14.95 28258

This is a dry-to-just-off-dry riesling that successfully spans a couple of food styles. You can drink it with poultry, seafood, white fish and smoked salmon, or exploit the subtle sweetness to pair it with spicy Asian-style dishes and sushi. Or you can just sip it on its own or serve it as an aperitif. The flavours are concentrated and defined, and very well complemented by brisk, zesty but friendly acidity.

NOTES

....

....

....

....

★ ★ ★ ★

Wayne Gretzky 'No. 99' Unoaked Chardonnay 2008

VQA NIAGARA PENINSULA $13.95 63826

This is a well-balanced chardonnay and, without any exposure to oak, the fresh and pure flavours show through. They're nicely layered and lifted by the generous, mouth-filling and refreshing texture. The back label suggests you pair it with paella, fettuccine alfredo or herbed pork tenderloin, and I can't think how you'd go wrong with any of those.

NOTES

....

....

....

....

SOUTH AFRICA

SOUTH AFRICA'S WINE REGIONS are mostly warm, which makes you think red wine. But they produce many very good-quality whites, too. The most popular variety used to be chenin blanc, but over the last ten years others (especially chardonnay and sauvignon blanc) have become more important.

Wines from official South African wine regions are called "Wines of Origin." In this list, the initials wo followed by a region indicate where the wine is from.

★ ★ ★ ★

The Beach House Sauvignon Blanc/Semillon 2011

WO WESTERN CAPE $9.95   122390

This is not a complicated wine, but if you're looking for a well-made, easy-drinking white, this might well be it. It shows the solid, bright flavours and crispness of sauvignon blanc and the rounder, more substantial weight of semillon, all nicely integrated. You can enjoy it on its own, but it goes well with many seafood and white fish dishes, as well as not-too-hot curries and Asian dishes.

NOTES
....
....
....
....

★ ★ ★ ★

Durbanville Hills Sauvignon Blanc 2011

WO DURBANVILLE $11.95   22251

This dry and medium-bodied sauvignon blanc will stand its ground against a lot that are priced significantly higher. It delivers concentrated flavours that are vibrant and substantial, and a texture that's mouth filling, smooth and very refreshing. It's a good choice when you're eating grilled white fish or seafood with fresh lemon, or lemon chicken.

NOTES
....
....
....
....

NEW!
★ ★ ★ ★ ½

Goats Do Roam White 2011

WO WESTERN CAPE $11.95   237313

Not only does this winery have a herd of goats, the name is also a play on Côtes du Rhône, the French wine region. As it happens, this dry, medium-weight wine is made from grape varieties typical to that region: viognier, roussanne and grenache blanc. Look for great depth of flavour here, with good complexity, and a refreshing and juicy texture. It's great with poultry, pork and rich seafood dishes.

NOTES
....
....
....
....

★ ★ ★ ½

Nederburg 'The Winemaster's Reserve' Sauvignon Blanc 2011

WO WESTERN CAPE $10.95   382713

Nederburg is an established (it's more than two centuries old) and big (production is about 13 million bottles a year) South African wine producer. In terms of a company's production, age is sometimes seen as an advantage but size as a problem. However, the company keeps quality up. This sauvignon blanc is zesty and refreshing, with good, clean flavours. It's made for food, so pair it with seafood or fish with a squeeze of lemon.

NOTES

....

....

....

....

NEW!
★ ★ ★ ★ ½

Petit Chenin Blanc 2011

WO STELLENBOSCH $12.95   266106

What a great combination! This is made from South Africa's signature white variety by one of the country's great winemakers, Ken Forrester. Everything's in place here: flavours that are concentrated, focused and defined, and a texture that's fresh and solid. This is fruity but serious. It goes well with poultry and pork and easily extends to slightly spicy Asian cuisine.

NOTES

....

....

....

....

NEW!
★ ★ ★ ★

Waka Waka Sauvignon Blanc 2011

WO PAARL $12.95   266494

The grapes used for this wine were grown on bush vines without supports, unlike most vines, which are trained along trellises or wires. The wine is full of flavour, with good complexity and depth, and the acidity is crisp and bright. This is a very attractive sauvignon blanc that goes well with seafood, shellfish and white fish, and pairs nicely with curries, too.

NOTES

....

....

....

SPAIN

SPAIN IS BEST KNOWN for its red wines and its sparkling wine, cava (see page 222). Much of the white table wine that Spain produces is consumed locally and never reaches international markets. However, that's changing as some of the larger wineries, like Torres, occasionally make white wines available in the Vintages section. With a bit of luck, some of these will eventually make their way to the LCBO General Purchase list.

The initials DO (*Denominación de Origen*) indicate a wine from one of Spain's designated wine regions. A higher-quality level, DOC (*Denominación de Origen Calificada*) has been awarded to only two regions: Rioja and Priorat.

Freixenet Mia Blanco 2010

SPAIN $11.95   269605

Freixenet is usually associated with sparkling wine (see pages 225–26) but this is a venture into a still wine. Made from four indigenous Spanish varieties, it's described on the label as "aromatic and fruity." It is, but it's also crisp and refreshing, the sort of wine that's great to drink on its own, or with spicy Asian dishes or well-seasoned seafood and chicken.

NOTES

....

....

....

....

★ ★ ★ ½   ## Marqués de Riscal 2011

DO RUEDA $10.75   36822

This is an attractive blend that's excellent for sipping on the patio or before a meal. Serve it with grilled or pan-fried white fish or roasted chicken. It's dry and medium bodied, with attractive and fairly concentrated fruit flavours. The texture is appealing, with richness from the fruit complemented by a refreshing crispness that makes it great by itself or with food.

NOTES

....

....

....

....

ARGENTINA

ARGENTINA IS THE WORLD'S FIFTH-LARGEST wine producer, but it began to make its mark on the world wine scene only a few years ago. Although we're seeing more and more quality and good-value wines from there, we haven't seen half of what Argentina can do. Wine producers (most located in the sprawling Mendoza region) make superlative reds and whites, and the reds are starting to get attention. Malbec, a red grape native to southwest France, has become Argentina's signature variety. Made in big and robust styles, the wine is a natural for beef, which just happens to be another of Argentina's major export products. But cabernet sauvignons and other reds can be just as impressive.

Argento Reserva Cabernet Sauvignon 2010

★ ★ ★ ½

MENDOZA $12.95   164764

Although best known for malbec, Argentina produces excellent cabernet sauvignons. This is a well-made cabernet that shows well-concentrated fruit flavours and a good, fresh texture from the acidity. It's dry and medium bodied, with a frame of easygoing tannins. This is an easy choice for grilled and braised red meats, meat loaf, burgers and ribs.

NOTES

....
....
....
....

Catena Malbec 2009

★ ★ ★ ★ ½

MENDOZA $19.95   478727

[Vintages Essential] Malbec from Argentina hit the wine world a bit like Australian shiraz did in the 1990s, and they often share a popular style: intense fruit flavours, generous texture and easygoing acidity. This malbec from Catena is a cut above many others. It delivers structure and balance, along with power and intensity. It's a great wine for full-flavoured, grilled red meats.

NOTES

....
....
....
....
....

Conquista Malbec 2010

NEW!
★ ★ ★ ★

MENDOZA $11.95   164772

Another day, another not-too-expensive Argentinian malbec. But wait! This one shows a more restrained flavour profile than many, it has quite extensive complexity and the texture is quite sleek as well as fresh. It's dry, mid-weight and lightly tannic, and it goes well with many foods. There are the usual red meats that Argentines adore, of course, but try it with pork and poultry, too.

NOTES

....
....
....
....

FuZion 'Alta' Reserva Cabernet Sauvignon 2010

NEW!
★★★★

MENDOZA $9.95   207357

Although known worldwide for malbec, Argentina also produces exceptional cabernet sauvignon. This is a very well-priced, entry-level example, but it delivers well across the board. It's lively and fresh, carries ripe and sweet fruit with some complexity, and has modest tannins. It's a very good choice for burgers, ribs and all kinds of red meat, grilled or braised.

NOTES

....

....

....

....

FuZion 'Orgánico' Malbec/Cabernet 2010

NEW!
★★★★

MENDOZA $12.95   127456

There are so many wines in the FuZion range that it's easy to become confused. Look for this one, though, as it delivers good quality across the board. It's full of ripe fruit, as you'd expect, and the tannins are moderate. It's also layered and plush—and, importantly, supported by a seam of fresh acidity. It goes well with Argentina's main meat: grilled beef.

NOTES

....

....

....

....

....

Graffigna 'Centenario' Reserve Malbec 2010

NEW!
★★★★ ½

SAN JUAN $12.95   230474

San Juan, where the grapes for this wine grew, lies just a couple of hours' drive north of Mendoza, Argentina's main wine-producing region. This malbec shows a lot of character for the price. Look for concentrated flavours that have complexity and structure, paired with the acidity to contribute a juicy texture. It's a good choice for grilled red meats and many other full-flavoured dishes.

NOTES

....

....

....

....

NEW!
★★★★
Graffigna 'Centenario' Reserve Shiraz 2008
SAN JUAN $12.95   164731

After stealing some of the popular red market with malbec, maybe
Argentina will give Australia a run for its money with shiraz, too. This
gutsy example, from the San Juan region (where more shiraz than malbec
is planted), shows a plush wine, with full-on fruit, good fruit-acid balance
and a fleshy, tangy texture. It's a great buy for burgers, ribs and red meats
for the barbecue in summer, or the grill in winter.

NOTES
....
....
....
....

NEW!
★★★★
La Linda Merlot 2010
MENDOZA $12.95   229849

Merlot is not as widely grown in Argentina as other red varieties, but it
makes good wine there, as it does elsewhere. La Linda's is chock full of
ripe, sweet fruit flavour with good complexity, and it has a tangy texture
from the balancing acidity. It's soft and smooth in texture, with minimal
tannins, and it goes well with red meats, pork and even poultry.

NOTES
....
....
....
....
....

NEW!
★★★★
La Linda Syrah 2009
MENDOZA $12.95   233651

La Linda is a brand of Luigi Bosca, a well-known Argentinian producer.
This is an affordable syrah that offers a break from the ocean of merlot
on the LCBO's shelves. Look for well-concentrated and focused flavours
with some complexity, and a round and tangy texture. You can't go wrong
pouring this syrah with red meats and many rich poultry dishes.

NOTES
....
....
....
....
....

Los Arboles Malbec 2010

NEW!
★ ★ ★ ½

MENDOZA $10.50   66696

This wine is named for the trees that provide a break against the cold wind that sweeps down from the Andes. It's a malbec that's full of sweet fruit flavours that are plush and forward, with a soft, easy-drinking texture and negligible tannins. Try it with dishes that have a sweet sauce or condiments, like barbecued ribs and hamburgers, or with spicy sausages straight from the grill.

NOTES

Masi Passo Doble 2010

NEW!
★ ★ ★ ★

TUPUNGATO $13.95   620880

This is a blend of malbec and corvina varieties, where the corvina grapes have been dried before being pressed. Drying eliminates some of the water so that the grapes have more concentrated and complex flavours. You can taste it in this wine, which shows intense and well-focused flavours and a rich, tangy texture. It goes well with a wide range of red meat dishes and hearty stews of all kinds.

NOTES

Misterio Malbec 2011

★ ★ ★ ½

MENDOZA $8.05   28803

This 100 percent malbec gets four months' aging in oak casks. The back label says it's "full of mystery," but I find it full of plush, ripe fruit flavours that are nicely balanced. It's dry and medium bodied and has a tangy texture. It's a very affordable choice for grilled red meats—great when you're having a crowd for a barbecue.

NOTES

Norton Cabernet Sauvignon 2011

NEW!
★ ★ ★ ½

MENDOZA $10.95   689996

Norton was founded by a British engineer who went to Argentina in the 1880s to build a railroad, married an Argentinian woman and received land as a present from her father. He planted the land in grapes, and now Norton is one of Argentina's largest wineries. This cabernet is full of ripe fruit, and is modestly complex and well balanced with fresh acidity. It's a great choice for burgers, pizzas and red meat dishes.

NOTES
....
....
....
....

Pascual Toso 'Limited Edition' Malbec 2010

NEW!
★ ★ ★ ★ ½

MENDOZA $14.95   162610

This is a step or two above many malbecs at this price. It has all the rich flavour that you expect of Argentinian malbec, but the integration and harmony of the components is notable. The fruit is ripe and focused, the acidity well calibrated and the tannins supple. Dry and medium bodied, it's a great choice for anything from a gourmet burger to a seasoned rack of lamb.

NOTES
....
....
....
....

Pascual Toso Merlot 2010

★ ★ ★ ★

MENDOZA $12.75   35188

The richness of this lovely merlot might come as a surprise the first time you taste it. The fruit-forward flavours are concentrated and focused, and the texture is smooth and mouth filling. It's on the fat side (low in acidity), so if you're sensitive to acidity, try this. Dry, more than medium bodied and lightly tannic, it goes wonderfully with well-seasoned red meats.

NOTES
....
....
....
....
....

Tilia Malbec 2010

★ ★ ★ ★

MENDOZA $12.95   160945

This Argentinian malbec is a cut above many of the rest at this price point. It has all the rich, concentrated flavours that you expect of malbec, but it adds very good degrees of complexity, as well as good structure and nice fruit-acid balance. It's great with hearty stews and red meats, especially with beef, Argentina's meat of choice.

NOTES
....
....
....
....
....

Trapiche Reserve Syrah 2010

NEW!
★ ★ ★ ★

MENDOZA $11.95   222281

What gives this syrah added points is that it's well balanced. So many wines at this price are full of fruit and short on almost everything else, but here you get a tangy, fresh texture from the acidity, and astringent dryness from the tannins. It's medium bodied and goes well with red meat dishes generally, but also with pork and poultry.

NOTES
....
....
....
....
....

Trivento 'Tribu' Malbec 2011

★ ★ ★ ★

MENDOZA $9.95   145284

From a winery named for the three winds that blow across Mendoza, this 100 percent malbec delivers across the board. The flavours are sweet, ripe and concentrated, with some complexity and structure, and they're lifted by a nice line of fresh acidity. It's quite dry and negligibly tannic, and goes well with burgers, grilled red meats and spicy sausages.

NOTES
....
....
....
....

Trumpeter Cabernet Sauvignon 2010

MENDOZA $12.95   218842

This is a big, quite dense cabernet sauvignon that's full of fruit kept on the leash by good structure and acidity. You'll find this mouth filling, with flavours that are ripe and plush but well defined and complemented by a full, round texture that has a tangy edge. The tannins are moderate. This goes very well with grilled or braised red meat or a juicy hamburger.

NOTES

....

....

....

....

....

AUSTRALIA

AUSTRALIA IS A REAL POWERHOUSE for red wine, and Australian shiraz dominated New World red wine exports for years. But although shiraz is king, other red varieties are very important—notably, cabernet sauvignon, merlot and pinot noir.

The most common geographical designation for Australian wine is South Eastern Australia. This isn't a state but a mega-zone that includes more than 90 percent of the country's wine production and most of its wine regions. The best-known smaller regions include Barossa Valley and McLaren Vale, both of which are represented in this list.

Angus the Bull Cabernet Sauvignon 2009

★ ★ ★ ★ ½

SOUTH EASTERN AUSTRALIA $19.85   602615

Now and again, a wine stands out from the herd, and Angus is one of them. It delivers generous, concentrated flavours that are complex and ripe, but well on this side of the fence that separates ripe from jammy. Full bodied and juicy, with relaxed tannins, it's a great partner for . . . beef, of course. But don't be cowed by this, and don't let me steer you away from serving Angus with other red meats.

NOTES

....

....

....

....

Clare Hills Shiraz/Cabernet 2008

NEW!
★ ★ ★ ★ ½

CLARE VALLEY $15.55   215103

Shiraz and cabernet used to be blended in France in the nineteenth century, but now Australia leads the way. This dry, medium-bodied example, from the prestigious Clare Valley, brings lovely, concentrated and layered flavours that are plush but restrained. The texture is fresh and quite juicy, the tannins are moderate, and it's a natural for lamb and other red meats, as well as full-flavoured cheeses.

NOTES

....

....

....

....

d'Arenberg 'd'Arry's Original' Shiraz/Grenache 2009

★ ★ ★ ★ ½

MCLAREN VALE $19.75   942904

[Vintages Essential] You find a lot of wines from the south of France that feature this blend, but this is in a no-nonsense, New World style that's quite different. It has intense and complex fruit flavours that are solid from front to back and leave a long finish. It's medium bodied and dry with a little tannic grip, and it has a rich and tangy texture. This is a perfect match for a well-seasoned rack of lamb, grilled medium rare at most.

NOTES

....

....

....

....

NEW!
★ ★ ★ ★

De Bortoli 'Deen de Bortoli' Vat 4 Petit Verdot 2008

SOUTH EASTERN AUSTRALIA $14.95   222265

Petit verdot is a red grape variety of Bordeaux, and it's usually used there as a tiny percentage (generally under 5 percent) in blends. But here it is used as a varietal, and it really struts its stuff. Look for intense and layered flavours with an equally big, mouth-filling texture. There's good acidity to keep things under control, and the tannins are forward. This needs big, intense food, so serve it with well-seasoned red meats.

NOTES

....

....

....

....

★ ★ ★ ★

De Bortoli 'Deen de Bortoli' Vat 8 Shiraz 2008

SOUTH EASTERN AUSTRALIA $14.95   621649

This is a nice change from many shirazes at this price level. It has all the full-on flavour you expect of shiraz, but it's well structured and has a lively, juicy texture that sets your palate up for food. It's dry and medium bodied, and although the alcohol is 14 percent, there's no sign of it in the flavour or texture. Drink it with grilled meats, like beef, lamb and even veal.

NOTES

....

....

....

....

....

★ ★ ★ ★

De Bortoli 'Deen de Bortoli' Vat 10 Pinot Noir 2009

SOUTH EASTERN AUSTRALIA $15.05   61622

This is a nicely made pinot noir in the successful 'Deen de Bortoli' series. It's definitely a New World style of pinot, with fairly plush fruit, but it has the structure and very good balance that gives it what you look for in the variety: versatility with food. It's medium bodied and dry, and goes well with grilled salmon, lamb, chicken, and turkey and cranberries.

NOTES

....

....

....

....

....

NEW!
★★★★
Fifth Leg Shiraz/Cabernet Sauvigon/Merlot 2009

WESTERN AUSTRALIA $16.00   212605

This is a terrific blend. It shows loads of plush, intense fruit that's consistent right through the palate, and brings it into harmony and balance with a seam of fresh acidity that lightens the intensity. The tannins are easygoing, and this is wine you can enjoy with well-seasoned, grilled or braised red meats.

NOTES

....

....

....

....

....

★★★★
Hardys 'Bankside' Shiraz 2010

SOUTH AUSTRALIA $14.95   436022

[Vintages Essential] This is a shiraz that lies comfortably between the in-your-face, jammy shirazes and those that are restrained and highly structured. It delivers ripe and quite plush flavours with a core of fruit sweetness. It's dry with quite gripping tannins, and has a full and generous texture that coats your mouth with flavour. Serve this with a rich meal, like lamb stew and sweet root vegetables.

NOTES

....

....

....

....

NEW!
★★★★
Hardy's 'Butcher's Gold' Shiraz/Sangiovese 2010

SOUTH AUSTRALIA $14.95   219139

Look for many more Australian wines made from Mediterranean varieties, like sangiovese, as plantings are expanding rapidly. Here the sangiovese brings high-toned fruit and acidity to the fruitiness of the shiraz, with very attractive results. The flavours have depth and complexity, and the texture is fresh and juicy. This is a very good choice for red meats and for well-seasoned dishes in general.

NOTES

....

....

....

....

Jacob's Creek Reserve Cabernet Sauvignon 2009

★ ★ ★ ★

COONAWARRA $16.95   91751

Jacob's Creek wines are now firmly regional, and what better Australian region to draw cabernet from than Coonawarra? This is a lovely, ripe, cool-climate style, where the fruit is solid but not in your face, and the acidity provides clean freshness. This is a wine you can enjoy glass after glass, with all kinds of red meats. Try it with well-seasoned, braised short ribs.

NOTES

....

....

....

....

Jacob's Creek Reserve Shiraz 2008

★ ★ ★ ★

BAROSSA VALLEY $16.45   665471

Jacob's Creek is an actual creek that meanders through the Barossa wine region. It's undistinguished as bodies of water go, but the little winery on its bank that first produced wine in 1850 did earn distinction. This Reserve Shiraz is solid from start to finish, with flavours of ripe fruit paired with a rich and tangy texture. It goes well with grilled lamb.

NOTES

....

....

....

....

....

NEW!
★ ★ ★ ★
Junior Shiraz 2010

MCLAREN VALE $16.30   183947

Junior is the younger sibling of Mitolo 'Jester' shiraz, which is also in this book (see page 109). Younger in vintage and a little less complex than 'Jester,' it nonetheless offers very good value. The flavours are concentrated and layered, the balance is right and a seam of fresh acidity carries everything along nicely. It goes well with red meats of all kinds, as well as hearty vegetarian risottos and paellas.

NOTES

....

....

....

Lenswood Hills Pinot Noir 2010

NEW!
★ ★ ★ ★

ADELAIDE HILLS $17.35   215095

The Adelaide Hills region is in South Australia, not too far from the city
of Adelaide, which is noted for its food and wine culture. This pinot noir,
which fits in perfectly, has balance as its keyword. On the one side, lovely
focused and layered fruit flavours; on the other, juicy acidity that suits it
to food. With relaxed tannins, this is a great choice for grilled duck breast,
roasted turkey and mushroom risotto.

NOTES
....
....
....
....

Lindemans 'Bin 45' Cabernet Sauvignon 2010

NEW!
★ ★ ★ ½

SOUTH EASTERN AUSTRALIA $11.95   119628

Like others in the 'bin' series (which refers to the bins that wines used
to be stored in before they were shipped from the winery), this cabernet
gets it right all the way through. The flavours are ripe, concentrated
and solid, and the fruit-acid balance is very good. There's nothing not to
like here, and it's an easy choice for burgers, red meats and many other
hearty dishes.

NOTES
....
....
....
....

Long Flat Cabernet/Shiraz 2006

★ ★ ★ ½

AUSTRALIA $11.95   212373

The 'Long Flat' here refers to a vineyard, but there's nothing flat about
the wine. It's a fruity and medium-bodied blend that delivers good, ripe
flavours, and a texture that's fresh and verges on juicy. This wine is tilted
toward food, and I suggest opening it when you're looking at hamburgers,
ribs, red meats and grilled spicy sausages.

NOTES
....
....
....
....
....

The Lucky Country Shiraz 2010

★ ★ ★ ★

BAROSSA VALLEY / MCLAREN VALE $15.85   145276

The lucky country is Australia and the lucky find is this shiraz, because it's a notch or two above many in a forest of shirazes. You'll find it has attractive, not too blowsy fruit, with complexity and structure, and good acid balance. Lightly tannic, it's a safe bet for grilled red meats and spicy sausages.

NOTES

....
....
....
....
....

McGuigan 'Black Label' Shiraz 2010

★ ★ ★ ½

SOUTH EASTERN AUSTRALIA $9.95   325787

Delivering a lot for a little has made this a popular shiraz. It boasts plenty of concentrated fruit and quite good complexity, and has a texture that's tangy and even vibrant, considering the density of the fruit. Dry and modestly tannic, it's a no-brainer for juicy burgers, barbecued ribs and well-seasoned red meats generally.

NOTES

....
....
....
....

McWilliam's 'Hanwood Estate' Cabernet Sauvignon 2009

★ ★ ★ ½

SOUTH EASTERN AUSTRALIA $14.95   214577

This is a successful cabernet sauvignon that achieves a nice balance of fruit, acidity and tannins. The flavours are concentrated and reasonably complex, the texture is refreshing and the tannins are drying but easily manageable. It's an excellent choice for gourmet burgers and for grilled or roasted red meats.

NOTES

....
....
....
....

McWilliam's 'Hanwood Estate' Shiraz 2010

★ ★ ★ ★

SOUTH EASTERN AUSTRALIA $14.95   610683

Many Australian shirazes in this price range taste very similar, so it's nice to come across one with some individuality. This has the layered ripe fruit flavours of a well-made shiraz, and some light oakiness from the barrels in which it was aged. It's medium bodied, has a slightly tangy texture and goes well with grilled lamb chops or a pepper steak.

NOTES

....
....
....
....
....

McWilliam's 'J. J. McWilliam' Cabernet/Merlot 2010

★ ★ ★ ½

SOUTH EASTERN AUSTRALIA $9.95   621599

The 'J. J. McWilliam' series is a value-priced line that bucks the trend of Australian wines reaching into the higher price points. This cabernet sauvignon/merlot blend delivers intense flavours that are not too complex, but certainly attractive. Decently balanced, it's a good choice for burgers, pizza and parties.

NOTES

....
....
....
....

Mitolo 'Jester' Shiraz 2009

★ ★ ★ ★ ½

MCLAREN VALE $21.95   659607

[Vintages Essential] 'Jester' takes its name from Richard Tarlton, a favourite clown of Queen Elizabeth I, and it celebrates humour and intellect. It also celebrates quality wine and wonderful value. This is an impressive shiraz that speaks to style all the way through, from the well-structured and extracted flavours, through the rich and refreshing texture, to the fine balance. Drink it with full-flavoured red meats like well-seasoned lamb, pepper steak or a great burger.

NOTES

....
....
....
....

Penfolds 'Koonunga Hill' Cabernet Sauvignon 2010

★ ★ ★ ★ ½

SOUTH AUSTRALIA $17.00 45625

Penfolds is one of the great names in Australian wine, not least because it produces Grange, the country's most sought-after wine. The 'Koonunga Hill' range of wines is dirt cheap in comparison, but they're all quality. This is a beautiful cabernet that has concentrated and well-defined flavours and a dense, tangy, refreshing texture. It's dry, with moderate tannins. Enjoy it with red meat cooked no more than medium rare.

NOTES

Penfolds 'Koonunga Hill' Shiraz/Cabernet 2010

★ ★ ★ ★ ½

SOUTH AUSTRALIA $16.95 285544

Although the shiraz/cabernet sauvignon blend is also made elsewhere, Australia has made its own, and this example shows the character well. Look for rich, ripe fruit that's sweet at the core, layers of complexity and a tangy, fresh texture from the underlying acidity. It's dry with moderate tannins and a great partner for grilled red meats.

NOTES

Penfolds 'Thomas Hyland' Shiraz 2010

★ ★ ★ ★ ½

SOUTH AUSTRALIA $19.95 611210

[Vintages Essential] This big, luscious shiraz is named for the son-in-law of Dr. Penfold, who founded the company. Thomas would be delighted to be associated with it. It's an assertive red with intense fruit flavours, and it has a texture that's plush, dense and tangy. Between medium and full bodied, it's a sheer pleasure to drink—especially with well-seasoned red meat, like lamb with garlic and rosemary.

NOTES

Peter Lehmann 'Clancy's Legendary Red' 2008

★ ★ ★ ★ ½

BAROSSA VALLEY $17.95   611467

Clancy's is just about a household name in Australia, where it has won many awards. It's a delicious blend of shiraz, cabernet sauvignon and merlot, and it delivers terrific depth and breadth of flavour, enhanced by plenty of complexity. Full bodied with a dense and juicy texture, it's dry and carries its tannins lightly. You just can't go wrong pouring this with hearty red meat dishes.

NOTES

....

....

....

....

Peter Lehmann Shiraz 2008

★ ★ ★ ★

BAROSSA VALLEY $19.95   672875

Peter Lehmann is one of the icons of the Australian wine industry, and his big, bold presence is reflected in some of his wines—like this one. It's a classic dry Barossa shiraz with full, ripe fruit flavours, nice complexity and a stylish, tangy texture. It's high in alcohol (14.5 percent) but it's well managed and balanced, and doesn't intrude into the flavours or texture. This is a perfect match for barbecued red meats.

NOTES

....

....

....

....

NEW!
★ ★ ★ ½

Peter Lehmann 'Weighbridge' Shiraz 2009

SOUTH AUSTRALIA $14.95   219170

'Weighbridge' refers to the weighing of grapes as they're brought from the vineyards to the winery. Sourced from locations in various parts of South Australia, this wine delivers the full fruit flavours you expect of Australian shiraz. But it's not one-dimensional—it has good balance and complexity and an attractive, tangy texture. It's a very good choice for a wide range of hearty red meat dishes.

NOTES

....

....

....

....

Red Knot Cabernet Sauvignon 2010

★ ★ ★ ★ ½

MCLAREN VALE $17.95 91702

It's not so much a knot on the label, as an impossibly tangled piece of . . . string? The wine itself is a lot easier to unravel. First you get very pleasant and complex aromas (if you bother to sniff it), then a mouthful of lovely, rich fruit that's concentrated, focused and layered. The tannins are supple, the balance is right on. What's not to like? And it's even better with red meat or a hearty mushroom risotto.

NOTES

....

....

....

....

Red Knot Shiraz 2010

★ ★ ★ ★ ½

MCLAREN VALE $17.95 619395

This wine has one of the more unusual closures. First you unwind the plastic tail (undo the knot, I suppose) and then the whole thing comes off. After playing with that, you get to taste the wine, which is much more fun. It's plush and densely flavoured, with a generous and smooth texture. There's some tanginess there, too, and it's well balanced. This goes nicely with well-seasoned red meats like barbecued ribs.

NOTES

....

....

....

....

Ringbolt Cabernet Sauvignon 2009

NEW!
★ ★ ★ ★ ½

MARGARET RIVER $19.95 606624

[Vintages Essential] Margaret River is one of the wine regions of Western Australia, an area that has developed a reputation for high-quality wines. This cabernet is one of them. You'll find it has concentrated and full-on flavours, but they're focused and complex and nicely balanced by the refreshing acidity. The tannins are ripe and supple, and this is a great choice for grilled, roasted or braised red meats.

NOTES

....

....

....

Rosemount Estate 'Diamond Label' Shiraz 2010

★ ★ ★ ★ ½

SOUTH EASTERN AUSTRALIA $15.95   302349

This is almost a classic Australian shiraz. It's been in the LCBO for many, many years, and the style has evolved nicely over time. It's all there—the rich, ripe flavours and the tangy texture that you expect. But it's not overbearing, not in your face. It's medium bodied with a dry, lightly tangy texture, has good structure and is excellent with grilled lamb chops or roasted lamb.

NOTES

....
....
....
....

Rosemount Estate 'Diamond Label' Shiraz/Cabernet 2010

★ ★ ★ ½

SOUTH EASTERN AUSTRALIA $11.95   214270

Like the others in this line, the shiraz/cabernet is from the huge South Eastern Australia wine zone, which covers the bulk of Australia's wine regions. The diversity of the area allows producers to source their grapes from many different regions. This blend offers solid flavours that are ripe and concentrated, and a mid-weight texture that's fruity and very lightly tannic. Open a bottle of this when you're serving hamburgers.

NOTES

....
....
....
....

NEW!
★ ★ ★ ★ ½

Tic Tok Cabernet Sauvignon 2009

MUDGEE / FRANKLAND RIVER $15.95   187179

From two smaller wine regions in two different states, this is a lovely cabernet sauvignon through and through. The balance is immediately striking, with well-focused and layered fruit on one dimension, fresh and clean acidity on another, and ripe, supple tannins making the third. The wine is fruity but well calibrated. It's a pleasure to drink with grilled or braised red meats.

NOTES

....
....
....
....

NEW!
★★★★

Tic Tok Shiraz 2009

FRANKLAND RIVER / MUDGEE $15.95   187187

The great-great-grandfather of the owner of this winery was a clockmaker, so . . . the Tic Tok range. The shiraz, from two small wine regions, shows plush and quite intense flavours right across the palate, moderate tannins and good fruit-acid balance. It's definitely built for bigger foods. Grilled red meats or a plate of well-seasoned lamb chops would be a natural combination.

NOTES

....

....

....

....

NEW!
★★★★ ½

Wolf Blass 'Grey Label' Shiraz/Cabernet 2009

ROBE / MOUNT BENSON $34.95   261487

A blend of varieties and wine regions (Robe is one of the country's newest official wine regions), this impressive shiraz/cabernet delivers a big punch of ripe fruit, but it's softened by complexity and balance. Look for layered and diverse flavours, a good seam of acidity underpinning the fruit and supple tannins. Still, it's a hefty number, and a candidate for full-on, well-seasoned lamb or beef.

NOTES

....

....

....

....

★★★★

Wolf Blass 'Red Label' Shiraz/Cabernet 2010

SOUTH EASTERN AUSTRALIA $14.95   311795

The shiraz/cabernet blend was made famous by Australia, and this example shows why it's been so successful. It's rich in layers of flavour that sweep into your mouth on a tangy tide. The fruit is ripe and sweet, but this is dry and medium bodied, with light tannins. It's an excellent choice when you're serving grilled or roasted red meats or hearty stews.

NOTES

....

....

....

....

Wolf Blass 'Yellow Label' Cabernet Sauvignon 2010

★ ★ ★ ★

SOUTH AUSTRALIA $16.95   251876

There was a time when no self-respecting restaurant would leave this off its wine list. It was everyone's standby for steak (and red meat in general) and, in fact, for any food. Taste it and you'll see the attraction. It's just well made and delivers above par in flavour, texture and finish. You'll find fruit-packed flavours and a full and tangy texture in this dry, medium-bodied cab.

NOTES

....

....

....

....

Wyndham Estate 'Bin 444' Cabernet Sauvignon 2009

★ ★ ★ ★

SOUTH EASTERN AUSTRALIA $15.45   110486

Wyndham Estate does things right, and achieves quality and value across the varietal board. This cabernet sauvignon presents flavours that have length, breadth and complexity, along with a texture that's rich, satisfying and refreshing. The tannins are present and manageable, especially when you drink this (as you might) with medium-rare beef or lamb, juicy burgers or an aged cheese, such as cheddar or Parmigiano Reggiano.

NOTES

....

....

....

....

Wyndham Estate 'Bin 555' Shiraz 2009

★ ★ ★ ★

SOUTH EASTERN AUSTRALIA $15.95   189415

Founded in 1828, Wyndham Estate is Australia's oldest operating winery. George Wyndham, an English immigrant, planted the country's first commercial shiraz vineyard. He had no idea what he was starting. This shiraz, harvested in the winery's 181st year, delivers plush fruit flavours and a generous, mouth-filling and refreshing texture. It's a great choice for roasted or grilled lamb.

NOTES

....

....

....

....

★ ★ ★ ★

Yalumba 'Y Series' Shiraz/Viognier 2009

SOUTH AUSTRALIA $15.05   624494

The inspiration to add viognier, a white grape, to shiraz comes from the northern Rhône Valley in France, where producers have long added a little viognier to give the aromas and flavours of their shirazes (syrahs) a lift. It sure works here, too. The aromas and flavours are lovely and complex, and the texture is rich and tangy. Medium-bodied and dry, this is an excellent choice for grilled lamb chops.

NOTES

....
....
....
....

NEW!
★ ★ ★ ½

[yellow tail] Reserve Shiraz 2010

SOUTH EASTERN AUSTRALIA $15.95   234609

Perhaps the subliminal attraction of [yellow tail] is that the wallaby on the label has a gold and orange tail. Its thighs are yellow, but [yellow thigh] doesn't seem as effective as a brand. This is a plump and fruity shiraz with some complexity in the flavours and good acidity, making for a tangy texture. It's easy drinking, and goes well with grilled red meats and gourmet burgers.

NOTES

....
....
....
....

AUSTRIA

AUSTRIA IS FAR BETTER KNOWN for its white wines than for its red, but the reds are coming on strong, and we should start to see more of them in Ontario in the next few years. Pinot noir is a popular variety, but zweigelt is also widely cultivated.

Zvy-gelt Zweigelt 2008

NIEDERÖSTERREICH $12.50   232348

The name (on what is one of the ugliest labels in the LCBO) tells you how to pronounce the grape variety. It's not well known outside central Europe, and here it makes a red with good flavours and an edgy, tangy texture. It's dry and medium weight, has drying tannins and goes well with burgers and barbecued ribs, as well as pork and many red meats.

NOTES

....

....

....

....

THE 500 BEST-VALUE WINES IN THE LCBO | 2013

BRITISH COLUMBIA

BRITISH COLUMBIA'S WINERIES—most of which are located in the Okanagan Valley—produce a lot of high-quality and well-priced red wine. Unfortunately, hardly any of it makes its way to Ontario.

The VQA (Vintners Quality Alliance) classification on British Columbia wine labels means that the grapes were grown in the region specified, and that the wine has been tested and tasted by a panel.

Mission Hill Reserve Cabernet Sauvignon 2009

★ ★ ★ ★ ½

VQA OKANAGAN VALLEY $22.95   653321

[Vintages Essential] Mission Hill helped put the Okanagan Valley wine region on the map, and the company's attention to detail has kept it in the forefront of British Columbia wine producers. This cabernet sauvignon is stylish and opulent. You'll find elegant fruit flavours and a rich and tangy texture. A bit more than medium bodied and dry, it goes nicely with well-seasoned red meats.

NOTES

....

....

....

....

CALIFORNIA

CALIFORNIA'S WINE INDUSTRY BEGAN in earnest in the 1850s, soon after the Gold Rush had subsided. The industry fell on hard times during Prohibition in the 1920s and early 1930s, but was given a boost when, in 1976, some California wines beat some of the best bordeaux and burgundies in a blind-tasting in Paris. California now accounts for 90 percent of the wine produced in the United States, and is fourth in world production after France, Italy and Spain.

California's varied growing conditions are suitable for many different grape varieties and wine styles. The state's signature grape is zinfandel (the excuse for many zin-fully bad puns), but cabernet sauvignon is more important. Other significant varieties are merlot, shiraz (syrah) and pinot noir.

Most of the value wines in this section are labelled "California," which means that producers can use grapes grown anywhere in the state. Important designated regions within the state include Napa Valley, Sonoma County and Paso Robles.

NEW!
★★★★

181 Merlot 2009

LODI $16.95   146548

This wine is named for the 181 clone of merlot, which is widely planted on the right bank of the Dordogne River in Bordeaux, the source of many prestigious merlots. The result here is quite elegant. It has all the fruit flavour and softness that you expect of merlot, but the texture has some sleekness and the tannins are fine and supple. Rather than pair this with red meat, try it with roast chicken or turkey.

NOTES
....
....
....
....

NEW!
★★★★

Aquinas Pinot Noir 2009

NAPA VALLEY $17.95   277657

It's actually named for St. Thomas Aquinas, for reasons outlined on the back label. The wine itself is less theological than stylish and compelling. It's fruit forward, but in a controlled way, with nice, layered complexity, a smooth and fresh texture and light tannins. This is an easy choice for roast chicken and turkey, mushroom risotto and paella, and it stretches to simple red meat dishes, as well.

NOTES
....
....
....
....

★★★★

Beringer 'California Collection' Cabernet Sauvignon 2010

CALIFORNIA $9.95   113001

This 'California Collection' cabernet sauvignon does what's intended: provides good quality at a very reasonable price. It's all solid fruit flavours that have good complexity and weight, and a texture that's satisfying and tangy. Dry and well balanced, it's a good choice for red meats, burgers and spicy sausages.

NOTES
....
....
....
....

★ ★ ★ ★ ½
Beringer 'Founders' Estate' Cabernet Sauvignon 2009
CALIFORNIA $18.95   634263

Beringer is Napa Valley's oldest, continuous wine producer, dating back to 1876. It stayed in business even during the dry days of Prohibition by making sacramental wine. This cabernet is delicious rather than spiritual, and delivers a medium body, an intense and juicy texture, and good solid fruit flavours. It's dry, the tannins are moderate and it goes very well with steak.

NOTES
....
....
....
....

NEW!
★ ★ ★ ★
Beringer 'Founders' Estate' Merlot 2009
CALIFORNIA $18.95   634255

The founders referred to here are the Beringer Boys, the brothers who established the winery in Napa Valley in the 1800s. This is a plush merlot with flavours that are concentrated, defined and solid from start to finish. It has just the right level of acidity, complementing the ripe fruit, and supple, easily approached tannins. Think of this when you're serving grilled red meats and similar hearty dishes.

NOTES
....
....
....
....

★ ★ ★ ★ ★
Beringer 'Knights Valley' Cabernet Sauvignon 2009
KNIGHTS VALLEY $34.95   352583

[Vintages Essential] This is a stunning wine, vintage after vintage. It achieves the feat of being both bold and stylish at the same time, which distinguishes many fine wines. The flavours are deep, broad and intricately layered, the texture is plump, plush and generous, and the acidity is beautifully handled. The tannins are still gripping, so you might decant it for two or three hours to enjoy with beef, grilled or roasted no more than medium rare.

NOTES
....
....

★ ★ ★ ★ ½

Bonterra Cabernet Sauvignon 2010

MENDOCINO COUNTY / LAKE COUNTY $19.95   342428

This is an organic wine, meaning that the grapes were grown without the use of chemical fertilizers or herbicides. This cabernet sauvignon includes a little merlot, syrah and other red varieties, and they add up to a delicious red with a full but sleek texture from the acidity. The flavours are focused and layered. This is a great cabernet for red meats and hearty stews.

NOTES

....
....
....
....
....

★ ★ ★ ★ ½

Cline Syrah 2009

SONOMA COUNTY $13.45   733758

The Sonoma Valley lies next to the better-known Napa Valley. In contrast to busy, commercialized Napa, Sonoma seems restfully rural. But there's nothing sleepy about the wines, as this classic Sonoma syrah shows. It has dynamic, rich flavour, a medium-to-full body, a refreshing texture and good tannic structure. It's great with grilled lamb or steak.

NOTES

....
....
....
....
....

★ ★ ★ ★

Cline Zinfandel 2010

CALIFORNIA $13.45   489278

This is a good example of a zinfandel made to go with food. Unlike too many high-octane, high-performance zins that leave food in the dust, this one has a refreshing texture (not a heavy, low-acid one) and the concentrated ripe flavours are layered. It's medium bodied and the very dry texture works well with its fruitiness. It's a natural for juicy hamburgers or other well-seasoned red meats.

NOTES

....
....
....
....

★ ★ ★ ★

Dancing Bull 'Vintage Blend' Zinfandel 2010

CALIFORNIA $12.95 669499

Although the dancing bull on the label occupies a smaller part than he did in the past, he still looks fairly happy, and he's choreographed a zin that stresses ripe fruit flavours over sheer power. The texture is substantial and plush, but it manages to be fresh and light on its feet . . . or hoofs. This is a zin you can happily pair with ribs or a steak with barbecue sauce.

NOTES

....
....
....
....
....

NEW!
★ ★ ★ ½

Deep Purple Zinfandel 2010

LODI $15.95 234401

Deep Purple is the brand (not the rock band) and deep purple is the colour. As you'd expect, it has intense and sweet, ripe flavours, but they're moderated here by judicious acidity. It's dry and more than medium in weight, and it goes well with grilled red meats, braised lamb, burgers and barbecued ribs.

NOTES

....
....
....
....
....

★ ★ ★ ★ ½

DeLoach 'Heritage Reserve' Cabernet Sauvignon 2010

CALIFORNIA $14.80 89250

The DeLoach style comes through clearly here: It's fruit forward, well structured and exceptionally well balanced. The fruit is ripe, sweet and well defined, intense without going near jamminess. The texture lifts the flavours and refreshes your palate, making this a great wine for food. It's medium weight and dry, with easygoing tannins, and excellent with roasted or grilled beef and lamb, or a veal chop.

NOTES

....
....
....

....

NEW!
★ ★ ★ ★ ½
DeLoach 'Heritage Reserve' Pinot Noir 2009
CALIFORNIA $15.75   220434

This is a very attractive pinot noir in a fruit-forward style. Look for fruit that's rich and full, with plenty of layered complexity. The acidity comes through very effectively, taming the fruit richness and adding some freshness to the texture. With soft and supple tannins, this is a good bet for grilled red meats and rich mushroom dishes.

NOTES

....

....

....

....

....

NEW!
★ ★ ★ ★
Fetzer 'Valley Oaks' Cabernet Sauvignon 2009
CALIFORNIA $12.80   336974

This is a very good mid-range, dry, medium-bodied cabernet that's simply well made and very attractive. It goes well with the usual cabernet suspects—red meats, burgers, grilled sausages—but extends to roasted pork and poultry. There's nothing paltry about the wine itself, which shows concentrated flavours, good complexity and structure, and a fresh texture.

NOTES

....

....

....

....

★ ★ ★ ★
Gnarly Head 'Cab' Cabernet Sauvignon 2010
CALIFORNIA $14.95   68924

The label shows a stylized and very gnarly grapevine, making you think this could be from old vines. There's no such claim, but the wine has the concentrated flavour you often expect from more mature vines. Look for intense, sweet fruit flavours here, with a generous texture and drying tannins. It's medium-to-full in weight, and goes with heavier dishes, like steak.

NOTES

....

....

....

....

Hahn Pinot Noir 2008

NEW!
★ ★ ★ ★

MONTEREY COUNTY $19.05   226555

This is distinctly in the style known as "New World," with the fruit upfront—and fruit that's ripe, with a sweet core, and complex and persistent right through the palate. It's paired with the fresh acidity that's the hallmark of successful pinot noir, and shows easygoing tannins. Ready to drink now, this goes well with roasted lamb, pork and poultry, as well as grilled salmon and hearty vegetarian dishes, like a mushroom risotto.

NOTES

....

....

....

....

J. Lohr 'Seven Oaks' Cabernet Sauvignon 2009

★ ★ ★ ★

PASO ROBLES $21.95   656561

Paso Robles is a region that has quickly earned a reputation for high-quality wines. This well-balanced cabernet sauvignon shows lovely, ripe fruit flavours that are well defined and layered, and accompanied by a seam of acidity that contributes an attractive tangy texture. The tannins are present but manageable, and this is a great choice for grilled or roasted red meats.

NOTES

....

....

....

....

Liberty School Cabernet Sauvignon 2009

★ ★ ★ ★ ★

PASO ROBLES $19.95   738823

[Vintages Essential] Skylar Stuck, export manager of Treana Winery (which makes Liberty School), describes this as "a step and a half above any other cab we've made." This is one of the great buys in the LCBO. It over-delivers on everything, with compelling, concentrated, ripe aromas and flavours, a generous, mouth-filling and tangy texture, sweet tannins and a long finish. It's a natural for rich red meat dishes.

NOTES

....

....

....

NEW!
★ ★ ★ ★ ½

Painter Bridge Cabernet Sauvignon 2010

CALIFORNIA $13.25   219113

This is a lovely cabernet, full of concentrated fruit and complexity, and light on its feet. The acidity is perfectly pitched and brings freshness to the wine, while the tannins are supple, drying and easily manageable. Everything is well balanced, and this is an excellent choice for roasted poultry, simple red meat dishes and moderately flavoured cheeses.

NOTES

....
....
....
....
....

NEW!
★ ★ ★ ★ ½

Parducci Sustainable Red 2007

MENDOCINO COUNTY $14.95   229740

Here's a real fruit salad of a wine, made from syrah, zinfandel, carignane, petite sirah, cabernet sauvignon and viognier. But it works! It really works. It's full bodied and a touch rustic, with intense and layered fruit flavours and a rich, tangy texture. The tannins are present and accounted for, but quite manageable, and it's a very good choice for well-seasoned red meats of all kinds. It's from the first carbon-neutral winery in the US.

NOTES

....
....
....
....

★ ★ ★ ★ ½

Ravenswood 'Old Vines Vintners Blend' Zinfandel 2010

CALIFORNIA $17.95   359257

[Vintages Essential] If there's such a thing as a classic California zinfandel, this wine, with its plush, ripe fruit flavours, might be it. But it's also dry and moderately tannic, and has an elegance you don't always find in high-octane zinfandels. This one is full flavoured, to be sure, but it's light on its feet and has a clean, fresh texture that makes it especially good for food. Open this, summer or winter, when you're serving grilled red meats.

NOTES

....
....
....

NEW!
★ ★ ★ ★

Raymond 'Family Classic' Cabernet Sauvignon 2010

NORTH COAST $18.95   269761

The North Coast appellation is a vast area that includes most of California's wineries. This cabernet is full of fruit and the flavours are solid from start to finish. It's dry and lightly tannic, lies between medium and full bodied and shows a fairly plush but refreshing texture. It's built for well-flavoured food, so try it with seasoned red meats and stews.

NOTES

....

....

....

....

★ ★ ★ ★ ★

Robert Mondavi Cabernet Sauvignon 2009

NAPA VALLEY $34.95   255513

[Vintages Essential] How much should you pay for a Napa cab? Only the fare shown on the meter. The tariff here is a bit more than you usually find in the LCBO, but—wow!—this is a delicious cabernet. It's elegant and stylish right through, with luscious and complex flavours. It's dry and medium bodied, with moderate tannins and a sleek and quite refreshing texture. Serve it with rack of lamb or other grilled red meat.

NOTES

....

....

....

....

★ ★ ★ ★

Robert Mondavi 'Private Selection' Cabernet Sauvignon 2010

CALIFORNIA $17.95   392225

The 'Private Selection' series is known for quality and value, and this cabernet sauvignon fits in seamlessly. The flavours are well extracted and nicely layered, the texture is generous and smooth but refreshing, and the tannins are firm and manageable. This is a natural for roasted or grilled red meats, but it extends to rich pasta dishes and aged cheeses such as cheddar, too.

NOTES

....

....

....

....

Robert Mondavi 'Private Selection' Pinot Noir 2010

★ ★ ★ ★

CALIFORNIA $17.95   465435

This pinot noir is a real pleasure to drink, and it lives up to the quality that the Mondavi name is associated with. You'll find it has quite intense and vibrant flavours of fresh, ripe fruit, with a smooth, easy-drinking texture and light tannins. Dry and medium bodied, it's a fine choice for grilled planked salmon, or for roasted turkey or chicken with cranberries.

NOTES

Rodney Strong Pinot Noir 2009

★ ★ ★ ★ ½

RUSSIAN RIVER VALLEY $24.95   954834

[Vintages Essential] Russian River Valley is a cool area of California that's earned a reputation for fine pinot noirs. This is a very good example that shows beautifully focused fruit that's layered and consistent, right through the palate. It's supported by bright acidity and framed by supple tannins. Everything is in order for grilled lamb, duck breast or roasted red meats.

NOTES

SKN Cabernet Sauvignon 2010

NEW!
★ ★ ★ ★

NAPA VALLEY $16.95   218834

SKN stands for Screw Kappa Napa, whatever that means. The cabernet is easier to understand. It delivers a mouthful of plush, very complex fruit that's rich and dense in flavour. The texture is quite big and fleshy, and it's supported by good acidity and framed by supple tannins. It's a generous cabernet that goes well with well-seasoned grilled red meats and hearty winter stews.

NOTES

Sledgehammer Zinfandel 2010
NEW!
★ ★ ★ ★

NORTH COAST $17.95   230466

The Sledgehammer brand was designed for men: a bold design, macho name and big wines (no rosé in the range, of course!). But you don't need to be brawny and inarticulate to enjoy the wines. This zinfandel is big, as zins tend to be, but it has complexity and structure and good balance. Still, better to pair it with a manly meal like steak or other red meat.

NOTES
....
....
....
....
....

Smoking Loon Cabernet Sauvignon 2010
★ ★ ★ ★

CALIFORNIA $14.95   65517

Why is this loon smoking? Because this is a smokin' cabernet? It's chock full of rich, sweet fruit flavours, and it has an attractive texture that's quite mouth filling, but still refreshing and good for food. The tannins are drying and manageable. Drink this with grilled red meats at the cottage while you're listening for the loons. Can't hear them? It's because they've taken up smoking and can't call with cigars in their beaks.

NOTES
....
....
....
....

Smoking Loon 'Old Vine' Zinfandel 2010
NEW!
★ ★ ★ ★

CALIFORNIA $14.95   272393

The vines of some grape varieties can produce fruit for a century or more. Zinfandel is one of them, although the vines that produced for this wine were not that old. Still, it has all the intensity and concentration associated with low-yielding older vines. The fruit is plush, the texture shows good balance and freshness, and the tannins are moderate. Hitch this up to well-seasoned red meat.

NOTES
....
....
....
....

Wente 'Southern Hills' Cabernet Sauvignon 2009

★ ★ ★ ★ ½

LIVERMORE VALLEY / SAN FRANCISCO BAY $16.95   301507

These regions near San Francisco were first planted with vines by Spanish missionaries in the 1760s. The Wente family arrived in the 1840s. Powerful, intense and full of layers of rich fruit flavour, this full-bodied cabernet delivers a texture that's mouth filling and refreshing. The tannins are firm but manageable. This is a great choice when you're eating red meat, grilled or roasted no more than medium rare.

NOTES

....
....
....
....

Woodbridge Cabernet Sauvignon 2010

★ ★ ★ ½

CALIFORNIA $12.95   48611

Woodbridge is a Robert Mondavi brand that's designed to give good quality at a good price—good value, in other words. And this cabernet does, with solid fruit flavours and nice balance. It's medium bodied and dry, has a soft, low-tannin texture, and goes very well with burgers and grilled red meats.

NOTES

....
....
....
....
....

CHILE

CHILE PRODUCES MANY OF THE BEST-VALUE red wines in the LCBO. They tend to be bold and full of flavour, and include carmenère (Chile's signature variety), cabernet sauvignon, merlot, shiraz (syrah) and pinot noir, as well as blends.

What makes Chile such a good source for quality red wine? Climate and location are the keys. Most Chilean wine regions are in warm, sun-soaked valleys. Maipo and Colchagua are two, and they're both well represented among the wines here. As Chile's wines gain the following they deserve and sales increase, expect the prices to do the same. In the meantime, enjoy Chile's reds for their great quality and value at lower prices.

NEW!
★ ★ ★ ½

35° South Cabernet Sauvignon/Merlot 2010

CHILE $12.95   218859

Your first mouthful of this blend is a big whack of ripe fruit, but
the acidity and tannins kick in quickly and rein the fruit in. It's still
concentrated and plush in flavour, but there's some juiciness from the
acidity and the tannins dry it out. The grapes for this were organically
grown. Try it with grilled red meats and hearty stews.

NOTES

★ ★ ★ ½

Caliterra Reserva Cabernet Sauvignon 2010

DO COLCHAGUA VALLEY $8.95   257329

This is a basic, uncomplicated cabernet sauvignon that presents solid fruit
flavours with moderate complexity, and good fruit-acid balance. It's quite
dry, with negligible tannins, and has a tangy texture. It's a good choice for
burgers and barbecued ribs, and generally any red meat from the grill.

NOTES

NEW!
★ ★ ★ ★ ★

Carmen Gran Reserva Cabernet Sauvignon 2009

DO MAIPO ALTO $16.75   358309

Alto Maipo is a sub-region of the Maipo Valley that's now recognized as
one of the best (if not the best) areas in Chile for cabernet sauvignon. It's
cooled by the Andean winds, and the cabernets are as fresh as they can be
powerful. This example shows impressive complexity, with concentrated
and defined fruit, and a sleek texture framed by supple tannins. It's a
natural for well-seasoned red meats.

NOTES

NEW!
★ ★ ★ ★

Carmen Reserva Cabernet Sauvignon 2009

DO COLCHAGUA VALLEY $11.25   78980

Look for intense flavours here, but don't expect a simple fruit bomb: it's decently complex and structured. Moreover, the acidity comes through nicely, endowing the wine with a tangy and fresh character that suits it for food. Dry and medium bodied, with easygoing tannins, it's a natural for red meats, juicy burgers and barbecued ribs.

NOTES

....

....

....

....

....

NEW!
★ ★ ★ ★

Carmen Reserva Carmenère 2010

DO COLCHAGUA VALLEY $11.25   169052

In Chile, carmenère was long thought to be a variant of merlot until it was identified in one of the vineyards of the Carmen winery, which makes this wine. (There's no relationship between Carmen and carmenère.) This example is full of concentrated fruit, and shows good balance and some complexity. It's plush and fruity, and goes well with red meats and grilled spicy sausages.

NOTES

....

....

....

....

★ ★ ★ ★

Casillero del Diablo Reserva Cabernet Sauvignon 2010

CENTRAL VALLEY $11.95   278416

Concha y Toro, one of Chile's major wine producers, came up with a winner in this Casillero del Diablo range, which offers very good value across the board. The cabernet sauvignon delivers a solid flavour profile, with quite good complexity and a nice tanginess in the texture. It's dry, with light-to-medium tannins, and is a natural for grilled red meats.

NOTES

....

....

....

....

....

Casillero del Diablo Reserva Carmenère 2010

DO RAPEL VALLEY $11.95   620666

Is it a coincidence that a wine named for "the devil's cellar" was given a product code that included the numbers 666? And what was it the devil called, when he tried to lure a victim into his cellar? "Carmenère!" This example of Chile's iconic grape is full of fruit power, but is well defined and textured. It's medium-to-full in body, and has an edgy tanginess that invites food. Send in a piece of grilled red meat.

NOTES
....
....
....
....

★ ★ ★ ★

Casillero del Diablo Reserva Malbec 2011

DO RAPEL VALLEY $11.95   94060

Here's additional proof that Argentina doesn't have a lock on making malbec in South America. From the other side of the Andes comes this very attractive dry, medium-bodied and well-balanced version. It delivers quite concentrated and complex flavours, supported by a lively texture, that cry out for food. Answer with grilled red meats, as they would in Chile (and Argentina).

NOTES
....
....
....
....

NEW!
★ ★ ★ ★

Casillero del Diablo Reserva Merlot 2007

DO RAPEL VALLEY $12.95   427088

Let's face it, there's a lot of boring merlot out there, made in a style that's fruity but without any structure or interest. This one presents a good tangy texture that suits it to food, and I'd suggest serving it with juicy burgers or with grilled red meats like lamb or steak. The flavours are fairly intense and nicely defined and, overall, it all holds together well.

NOTES
....
....
....
....
....

Casillero del Diablo Reserva Shiraz 2010

★ ★ ★ ★

RAPEL VALLEY $11.95   668055

This range of wines is named for a cellar at the Concha y Toro winery.
The story goes that in order to deter workers from going into the cellar to
drink wine, the owner told them it was inhabited by the devil. Too bad
for them if they missed out on the likes of this. It's an intensely flavoured,
well-balanced, dry, tangy-textured, lightly tannic red, and it goes well
with barbecued red meats.

NOTES

Concha y Toro 'Marques de Casa Concha' Cabernet Sauvignon 2010

★ ★ ★ ★ ½

DO MAIPO VALLEY $19.95   337238

[Vintages Essential] Concha y Toro produces huge volumes of quality
wine, but this is one of their limited-production brands. The grapes come
from a single vineyard (always considered a plus) and the wine is oak-aged
for 14 months. What you get for a very good price is an elegant, well-
structured red with layers of flavours and a superlative texture. Serve it
with a good cut of red meat, cooked no more than medium rare.

NOTES

Concha y Toro 'Xplorador' Carmenère 2010

NEW!
★ ★ ★ ½

DO CENTRAL VALLEY $9.95   177816

It's not a very complicated carmenère, but it captures the rich fruitiness
of the variety and harnesses it to the acidity that translates into attractive
juiciness. It's fruit forward and medium bodied, and you can't go wrong
serving this with burgers, barbecued ribs and grilled red meats.

NOTES

138

Cono Sur Pinot Noir 2011

★ ★ ★ ★ ½

CENTRAL VALLEY $10.95 341602

Cono Sur is by far Chile's biggest producer of pinot noir. This one has the intense flavour you expect from a Chilean wine, but it's subtle enough to capture the classic textures and character of the variety. Look for concentrated flavours and a lively, food-friendly texture. Dry and medium bodied, it has light tannins and goes very well with grilled salmon or lamb.

NOTES

....

....

....

....

....

Cono Sur Reserva Cabernet Sauvignon 2010

NEW!
★ ★ ★ ★

MAIPO VALLEY $12.95 218883

The Maipo Valley is the source of many of Chile's great cabernet sauvignons. This is a less expensive (but very well-made) example that shows the intense and complex fruit that's typical of the region. It has a dense, full-bodied and tangy texture, and good acid balance, and it goes very well with full-flavoured dishes like well-seasoned lamb and pepper steak.

NOTES

....

....

....

....

....

Cono Sur Reserva Syrah 2010

NEW!
★ ★ ★ ★

COLCHAGUA VALLEY $12.95 221820

The label features a bicycle in recognition of Cono Sur's workers who cycle to work each day. Whether you cycle, walk or drive, pick up a bottle of this for your next meal of grilled lamb, or roasted turkey or pork. Dry and medium bodied, it features lovely flavours of ripe fruit, with good layered complexity and a seam of bright acidity that gives it a fresh, clean texture.

NOTES

....

....

....

....

Cono Sur Shiraz 2007

★ ★ ★ ★ ½

COLCHAGUA VALLEY $9.95   64295

This is a shiraz-dominant blend, with malbec, carmenère and cabernet sauvignon playing minor roles. The result is a medium-bodied and dry red with rich flavours that are dense and (for this price) remarkably complex. It has moderate tannins and a juicy texture. This is a very good buy and a great choice for grilled red meats, burgers and hearty vegetarian stews.

NOTES

....

....

....

....

....

Errazuriz 'Max Reserva' Shiraz 2008

★ ★ ★ ★ ½

ACONCAGUA VALLEY $17.95   335174

If you want to see why some wines are labelled "syrah" and others "shiraz" (they're the same grape variety), try this and the next wine together. This is a more fruit-forward style, with plush, dense and layered flavours. It retains very good balance and complexity, though, and goes well with well-seasoned red meats, like garlic/rosemary lamb and pepper steak.

NOTES

....

....

....

....

....

NEW!
★ ★ ★ ★ ½

Errazuriz 'Max Reserva' Syrah 2009

ACONCAGUA VALLEY $17.95   614750

This is a very attractive, full-bodied syrah delivering layered and concentrated flavours that are consistent right through the palate and hang on afterward. It's well structured and the fruit is balanced by good acidity that translates to a tangy, almost juicy texture. It's a natural for red meats, hearty stews and pastas, and many gourmet burgers.

NOTES

....

....

....

....

....

MontGras Reserva Cabernet Sauvignon 2011
★ ★ ★ ★ ½

DO COLCHAGUA VALLEY $11.95   619205

This is an impressive cabernet, full of rich, plush, concentrated fruit that's layered and shows good structure. It's full bodied and dry, with moderate tannins and a texture that manages to be plump and mouth filling, yet fresh at the same time. Think of this when you're serving well-seasoned, grilled or roasted red meats.

NOTES

....

....

....

....

....

MontGras Reserva Carmenère 2010
NEW!
★ ★ ★ ★

DO COLCHAGUA VALLEY $11.95   178624

One of the challenges of carmenère is to get it ripe, as it's a late-ripener that needs a long, warm growing season. The grapes in this wine found it, and they express it in ripe, sweet fruit flavours with good complexity. The texture is full and tangy. This is a red you can serve with red meats, burgers and spicy sausages off the grill.

NOTES

....

....

....

....

....

Pérez Cruz Reserva Cabernet Sauvignon 2010
★ ★ ★ ★ ★

DO MAIPO ALTO VALLEY $13.45   694208

[Vintages Essential] Vintage after vintage, this opulent cabernet sauvignon, from Chile's key cabernet region, is full of delicious, layered flavours. You can smell the rich aromas as you pour the wine into your glass. The texture is full, smooth and generous. For all its complexity, this is a dry wine with moderate tannins. It's perfect with well-seasoned red meat, like lamb with garlic and rosemary.

NOTES

....

....

....

....

NEW!
★ ★ ★ ★

Santa Carolina Reserva Cabernet Sauvignon 2010

DO COLCHAGUA VALLEY $12.00   275925

This is a gutsy cabernet, full of fruit that's dense and layered, and shot through with a seam of acidity that lightens and freshens the texture. The balance is good—it's light on its feet for fruit this weighty—and the tannins are drying. You'll want food with heft for this cabernet, so think of well-seasoned lamb or a pepper steak.

NOTES
....
....
....
....
....

★ ★ ★ ½

Santa Carolina Reserva Merlot 2010

COLCHAGUA VALLEY $10.00   324590

Many of the best-value wines come from regions that are undervalued, and Chile still falls into that category, despite the popularity of its wines. This merlot is a good example. It delivers tangy flavours that are concentrated and quite complex, and a solid, spicy texture. Medium-bodied, dry and moderately tannic, it's well made and a great choice for a wide range of well-seasoned meat and vegetarian dishes.

NOTES
....
....
....
....

★ ★ ★ ★ ½

Santa Digna Reserve Cabernet Sauvignon 2009

CENTRAL / CURICÓ VALLEY $14.95   177451

[Vintages Essential] From two of Chile's sun-soaked wine regions, this 100 percent cabernet delivers rich, plush and layered flavours, complemented and reined in by acidity that translates as a tangy texture. Dry, with moderate and supple tannins, it goes well with seasoned red meat, like a New York strip loin and a shake or two of steak spice.

NOTES
....
....
....
....

Santa Rita Reserva Cabernet Sauvignon 2009

★ ★ ★ ★

DO MAIPO VALLEY $13.95 253872

Santa Rita has one of the most beautiful estates in Chile, but you get only a hint of it from the sketch on the bottle's label. But the wine inside is the important thing. This is a very attractive cabernet sauvignon from one of Chile's premium cabernet regions. With quite intense flavours, and a texture that's complex, layered and tangy, this dry and medium-bodied red is a very good choice for grilled or roasted red meats.

NOTES
....
....
....
....

NEW!
★ ★ ★ ★

Santa Rita Reserva Carmenère 2009

DO RAPEL VALLEY $13.95 177774

As you would expect from carmenère, this shows concentrated fruit flavours. But it's no mindless fruit-bomb, because the ripe and sweet fruit is nicely calibrated, with some complexity, and it's well balanced with the acidity. Lightly tannic, this is a red that goes well with well-seasoned red meats. It's a popular summer choice for barbecues, and in winter it's a natural for hearty stews.

NOTES
....
....
....
....

FRANCE

FRANCE IS THE WORLD'S LARGEST wine producer, and one of the most important. It has scores of wines in the LCBO. For many years French wine was widely believed to be the best in the world, and bordeaux and burgundies were held up as the only wines worth drinking if you wanted to taste excellence. That's no longer so, as wine lovers have discovered the great wines made elsewhere. However, France continues to make high-quality and value-priced wine, as this list shows.

French wine labels display a few terms worth knowing. Wines labelled Appellation d'Origine Contrôlée (abbreviated AOC in this book) or Appellation d'Origine Protégée (AOP) are wines in the highest quality classification in France. They're made under tight rules that regulate aspects like the grape varieties that can be used in each region.

Wines labelled Vin de Pays or IGP (Indication Géographique Protégée) are regional wines made with fewer restrictions. They must be good quality, but producers have much more flexibility in the grapes they can use and how much wine they can make. Vins de Pays d'Oc (the ancient region of Occitanie) wines are by far the most important of the Vins de Pays wines.

★ ★ ★ ★

Albert Bichot 'Vieilles Vignes' Bourgogne Pinot Noir 2010

AOC BOURGOGNE $15.95 166959

Vieilles vignes refers to "old vines." There's no standard definition of "old" in any wine law, but as vines age they produce fewer and more intensely flavoured grapes, so producers like to highlight them. The flavours in this pinot are well concentrated and quite complex, and they're complemented by juicy acidity. Dry and lightly tannic, it's a very good choice for mushroom risotto, duck, lamb and roast turkey.

NOTES

....
....
....
....

NEW!
★ ★ ★ ★ ½

Antoine Moueix Merlot 2010

AOC BORDEAUX $12.95 245860

This is a delicious merlot from Bordeaux's Right Bank—the region where most merlot is planted. Look for a juicy and refreshing texture, with defined and well-focused fruit flavours. It's dry with quite firm tannins, and you can enjoy it with roasted or grilled red meats, pork, game and even poultry.

NOTES

....
....
....
....
....

★ ★ ★ ★ ½

Antonin Rodet Côtes du Rhône 2010

AOC CÔTES DU RHÔNE $12.95 8979

Antonin Rodet started off making wine in Burgundy in 1875, and the winery now produces wines under various labels in many other French regions. This côtes du Rhône has a very attractive texture: juicy and generous and ideal for food. The flavours have good depth, and the wine is dry and medium bodied, pitched just right for your meal, especially veal or lamb, but turkey or chicken, too.

NOTES

....
....
....
....

Bouchard Aîné & Fils Beaujolais Supérieur 2010

NEW!
★ ★ ★ ½

AOC BEAUJOLAIS SUPÉRIEUR $11.95 9431

Beaujolais supérieur is made according to slightly more stringent rules than simple beaujolais. You'll find that this one offers bright fruit that's solid through the palate, and a vibrant texture from the good acid-fruit balance. The tannins are negligible, and this makes a good wine to serve with roast chicken, turkey and ham.

NOTES

Bouchard Père & Fils 'La Vignée' Pinot Noir 2009

★ ★ ★ ★

AOC BOURGOGNE $16.95 605667

If you're looking for a quite stylish red to go with turkey and cranberries, roasted chicken, baked ham or summer salads, this pinot noir is an excellent candidate. It's made in the understated style often found in Burgundy. Don't be put off by the light colour; the flavours are nicely concentrated, with quite good complexity. It's dry, with moderate and manageable tannins, and well structured.

NOTES

Calvet 'Réserve des Remparts' Saint-Émilion 2010

★ ★ ★ ★

AOC SAINT-ÉMILION $18.95 31898

Saint-Émilion is one of the best-known appellations of Bordeaux. It's on the right bank of the Dordogne River, where the dominant grape variety is merlot and, sure enough, this is mostly merlot. Medium weight and dry, it has solid flavours, decent complexity and a fairly refreshing texture. It's a great partner for grilled and roasted red meats.

NOTES

Calvet Réserve Merlot/Cabernet Sauvignon 2010

★ ★ ★ ★

AOC BORDEAUX $13.95   44032

Here's a generic bordeaux—which means the grapes can be sourced from any appellation within the larger Bordeaux appellation—that really delivers for the price. The fruit is solid and nicely layered, the texture is generous and refreshing, and the balance is very good. The tannins are gripping firmly at present, and you can hang on to it for a year or two, but it goes well now with medium-rare red meats, or cheese like aged cheddar.

NOTES

....
....
....
....

Château Bel Air 2010

★ ★ ★ ★

BORDEAUX $11.95   665430

This medium-bodied blend of merlot, cabernet franc and cabernet sauvignon presents attractive and understated flavours. With a quite crisp texture and some tannic grip, it leaves your mouth dry but refreshed. It's a good, inexpensive choice for roast chicken, but it will also go well with turkey and cranberries, and with roast pork and many red meat dishes.

NOTES

....
....
....
....
....

Château de Courteillac 2010

★ ★ ★ ★ ½

AOC BORDEAUX $11.95   360552

This is a merlot-dominant blend, with contributions from cabernet sauvignon and cabernet franc. It's a solid, well-made red with concentrated flavours, some complexity and very good balance. Medium bodied and dry, with light tannins, it's very versatile with food, and will go well with many red meat, poultry and pork dishes.

NOTES

....
....
....
....
....

NEW!
★★★★

Château Ducla 2008

AOC BORDEAUX SUPERIEUR $14.95   255067

Ducla is a corruption of "Douglas," the name of a former owner of the fourteenth-century building on the winery property that's shown on the label. This is a blend of cabernet sauvignon and merlot, and it shows solid fruit from start to finish, good complexity and concentration, and effectively balancing acidity. The tannins are moderate and drying, and it's a very good choice for roast beef and other red meats.

NOTES

....

....

....

★★★★

Château Pey la Tour 2007

AOC BORDEAUX $14.45   264986

This well-made merlot/cabernet sauvignon blend is a generic bordeaux, or what used to be called an ordinary claret. You can see what has been so attractive for so long: well-defined fruit flavours and acidity, great balance, and moderate and manageable tannins. It's dry and medium bodied, and a great match for roasted red meats and older cheddar.

NOTES

....

....

....

....

....

★★★★½

Château Pey la Tour 'Réserve du Château' 2007

AOC BORDEAUX SUPÉRIEUR $19.95   925859

[Vintages Essential] Bordeaux has special status among wines, but you don't always need to take out a second mortgage to buy a good one. This merlot-dominant blend (89 percent, with 8 percent cabernet sauvignon and 3 percent petit verdot) is smooth and clean textured, with complex and concentrated flavours. It's medium bodied and dry with firm tannins, and has very good balance. It's a lovely wine and an excellent dancing partner for red meats.

NOTES

....

....

....

....

Château Saint-Germain 2008

AOC BORDEAUX SUPÉRIEUR $14.45 152587

You don't need to break the bank to enjoy a drinkable bordeaux. This one is well made, and shows a fresh, restrained texture and well-calibrated fruit flavours. It's dry and medium bodied, and goes very well with roast beef (and other red meats), and it will also extend to pork and poultry.

NOTES
....
....
....
....
....

★★★★

Château Timberlay 2009

AOC BORDEAUX SUPÉRIEUR $15.95 30072

This is a blend of merlot (80 percent) with 10 percent each of cabernet sauvignon and cabernet franc. The result is a red with very attractive fruit, in a restrained and structured style that's both solid and refreshing. The tannins are present and drying, but they're easily managed. This is an obvious choice for roast beef and for red meats in general, and it also goes well with older cheddar cheese.

NOTES
....
....
....
....

★★★★★

E. Guigal Côtes du Rhône 2009

AOC CÔTES DU RHÔNE $16.95 259721

[Vintages Essential] There's so much mediocre côtes du Rhône about that it's important to know which wines offer the best quality and value. There's no doubt at all that this, from one of the most respected producers in the Rhône Valley, is one of them. It carries its concentrated flavour with lightness and elegance, and the tangy texture is stylish. Medium bodied, astringently dry and moderately tannic, it's an excellent choice for red meats.

NOTES
....
....
....
....

François Labet 'Dame Alix' Côtes du Rhône 2010

★ ★ ★ ★

AOC CÔTES DU RHÔNE $11.45   630657

This is a blend of grenache, syrah and mourvèdre, three of the classic grapes of this region, which spreads across a broad swath east of the River Rhône near the Mediterranean. The wine has quite solid flavours, decent complexity and a slightly tangy texture. It's dry and medium bodied with moderate tannins. Drink it with pasta in tomato sauce, or with roast chicken or turkey (with cranberries).

NOTES
....
....
....
....

NEW!
★ ★ ★ ½

Hob Nob Merlot 2010

IGP PAYS D'OC $11.95   184077

The Pays d'Oc is a sprawling region in southern France that used to make millions of litres of cheap wine for domestic consumption. There's still some of that, but also a lot of good quality wine, like this merlot. Look for flavours that hold right through the palate, very good balance and relaxed tannins. It goes well with burgers, red meats and hearty stews.

NOTES
....
....
....
....
....

La Fiole du Pape Châteauneuf-du-Pape

★ ★ ★ ★

AOC CHÂTEAUNEUF-DU-PAPE $35.75   12286

[Non-vintage] You can't miss the bottle. It's gnarled and twisted, with a rough, gritty texture, as if it's been in a fire. But the wine's in very good shape. It's a stylish red that has good structure and food-friendly balance. Look for concentrated flavours with spicy accents and a tangy texture. It's medium bodied and dry, with moderate tannins. Serve it with grilled or roasted red meats.

NOTES
....
....
....
....

NEW!
★ ★ ★ ★
Laurent Miquel 'L'Artisan' Languedoc 2008

AOC LANGUEDOC $13.55   265918

This blend of syrah and grenache hails from the south of France.
Completely unoaked, it shows vibrant and solid fruit flavours that flow
consistently across the palate and are harnessed to a nice line of acidity
that makes the wine refreshing and tangy. This is a very good choice for
burgers and ribs, as well as for grilled and roasted meats generally.

NOTES
....
....
....
....
....

★ ★ ★ ½
La Vieille Ferme Ventoux 2010

AOC VENTOUX $11.75   263640

This is a blend of four southern French grape varieties—grenache, syrah,
carignan and cinsault—grown on the slopes of Mont Ventoux. They find
cooler conditions there, and the flavours here are concentrated and rich,
but not too intense. The texture is tangy, and you'll feel drying tannins.
You might want to tame them by drinking this with red meat, cooked
medium rare at most, or with aged hard cheese, like two-year-old cheddar.

NOTES
....
....
....
....

NEW!
★ ★ ★ ★
Les Jamelles Merlot 2010

VIN DE PAYS D'OC $12.95   245324

Merlot, one of the main red grapes of Bordeaux, is planted throughout the
world. The vines that produced this are fairly close to home, in southern
France, and they've come up with a style that's plush and rich in texture
and flavour. Look for good concentration, diversity of nuances and very
good acid-fruit balance. It's a no-brainer for red meats, but it extends to
pork, too.

NOTES
....
....
....
....

Louis Bernard Côtes du Rhône Villages 2010

NEW!
★ ★ ★ ★

AOC CÔTES DU RHONE VILLAGES $14.10   391458

The appellation means that the wine comes from villages within the Côtes du Rhône that are recognized as making superior wine. This one is mostly a blend of grenache and syrah, and it delivers lovely flavours that are focused and consistent right through the palate. Look for a refreshing texture and easygoing tannins. Drink this with red meats, pork, veal and well-seasoned sausages.

NOTES
....
....
....
....

Louis Jadot Bourgogne Pinot Noir 2009

★ ★ ★ ½

AOC BOURGOGNE $20.55   162073

Pinot noir is the signature grape of Burgundy, where it's made in many (often subtly different) styles. This example is affordably mid-range. It's medium bodied and very dry, with nicely managed fruit that delivers consistent flavours from start to finish. The tannins are easygoing, and the acidity adds a refreshing texture. It goes well with grilled salmon, poultry, pork and tomato-based vegetarian dishes.

NOTES
....
....
....
....

Louis Jadot 'Combe aux Jacques' Beaujolais-Villages 2010

★ ★ ★ ★

AOC BEAUJOLAIS-VILLAGES $15.95   365924

[Vintages Essential] Light in tannins, beaujolais (which is made from the gamay variety) is often a good choice for anyone who finds that red wines lead to a headache. This one is quite classic: medium bodied and dry with bright fruit flavours, some complexity and a vibrant and refreshing texture. You can serve it slightly chilled, especially in the summer, with roasted or grilled chicken or with roasted turkey.

NOTES
....
....
....
....

★ ★ ★ ★ Louis Latour Pinot Noir 2010

AOC BOURGOGNE $18.95   69914

This is a reliable red burgundy, now labelled pinot noir to help consumers who buy by grape variety, not wine region. It's in one of the classic burgundy styles: fairly light in colour, but with surprising depth and complexity in the flavours, a tangy and refreshing texture and drying tannins. It's a great choice for roasted poultry and cranberries, or for grilled salmon.

NOTES

....
....
....
....

NEW! ★ ★ ★ ★ ½ Mommessin 'Les Épices' Châteauneuf-du-Pape 2009

AOC CHÂTEAUNEUF-DU-PAPE $29.75   42242

Châteauneuf-du-Pape is an iconic appellation in the southern Rhône Valley, near Avignon. The wines can be made from many different varieties, but most, like this one, draw mainly on grenache. Here you'll find richness and complexity of flavour, big body and real depth to the smooth texture. The tannins are firm but manageable, and this calls for food with heft, like lamb and beef.

NOTES

....
....
....
....

NEW! ★ ★ ★ ½ Ogier 'Heritages' Côtes du Rhône 2010

AOC CÔTES DU RHÔNE $12.95   635849

This is a solid and reliable southern Rhône blend of grenache, syrah and mourvèdre. There's plenty of flavour here, with some complexity and structure. It's dry, medium bodied and nicely balanced, and has a good tangy texture and moderate tannins. Try it with grilled or roasted red meats, paella and coq au vin.

NOTES

....
....
....
....

NEW!
★ ★ ★ ★
Patriarche Pinot Noir 2010
VIN DE PAYS D'OC $10.45   622649

The big Pays d'Oc wine region runs along France's western Mediterranean
coast. It's fairly warm during the growing season, and not the sort of
climate in which you'd expect cool-climate-loving pinot noir to thrive.
But here, concentrated flavours are well complemented by acidity to give a
tangy and refreshing texture. Dry and medium bodied, it's a great choice
for duck, lamb or mushroom-based vegetarian dishes.

NOTES
....
....
....
....

★ ★ ★ ★ ★
Perrin & Fils 'Les Sinards' Châteauneuf-du-Pape 2009
AOC CHÂTEAUNEUF-DU-PAPE $36.75   926626

[Vintages Essential] 'Les Sinards' is a sort of junior Château de Beaucastel,
an iconic wine from this region, but it surrenders nothing to quality.
Made from grenache (70 percent), as well as syrah and mourvèdre (in
equal parts), this is simply opulent, with fleshy, plush and layered fruit,
finely tuned acidity and supple tannins. From an excellent vintage, this
goes well with lamb and other red meats, suitably seasoned.

NOTES
....
....
....
....

★ ★ ★ ★ ★
Perrin Réserve Côtes du Rhône 2009
AOC CÔTES DU RHÔNE $14.75   363457

[Vintages Essential] There's tremendous value in this bottle, vintage after
vintage. It's a blend of grenache, syrah, mourvèdre and cinsault made by
the producer of Château de Beaucastel, an iconic Châteauneuf-du-Pape.
This côtes du Rhône delivers rich, luscious flavours with an astonishingly
intense, smooth and mouth-filling texture. Dry and well structured, with
good tannic grip, it's a great choice for grilled or roasted red meats.

NOTES
....
....
....

NEW!
★ ★ ★ ★

Philippe de Rothschild Cabernet Sauvignon 2010

IGP PAYS D'OC $10.95   407551

This is bold and concentrated, and it's a step up in complexity and style from most reds at this price. The fruit is layered and defined, the fruit-acid balance is very good and there are quite firm tannins framing everything. Dry and a bit more than medium bodied, it looks very good for grilled red meats, spicy sausages and burgers.

NOTES

....
....
....
....
....

NEW!
★ ★ ★ ★

Philippe de Rothschild Merlot 2010

IGP PAYS D'OC $10.95   407544

This is a big, chunky merlot with very attractive juiciness that suits it to a wide range of food. Try it with grilled or braised red meats, gourmet burgers and grilled or roasted pork. It delivers quite dense, nicely layered flavours supported by fresh acidity, and the tannins are drying and moderate.

NOTES

....
....
....
....
....

NEW!
★ ★ ★ ★ ½

Pigmentum Malbec 2010

AOC CAHORS $13.95   255182

France's Cahors region is the home of malbec, and the name 'Pigmentum' recognizes the deep colour, or pigment, of the variety. This is a dark wine, with flavours that are also deeply concentrated, as well as layered and nicely structured. It has a clean, tangy texture, and it's an easy choice when you're serving grilled or roasted red meats or well-flavoured aged cheeses.

NOTES

....
....
....
....

NEW!
★ ★ ★ ★ ½

Rigal 'Les Terrasses' Malbec 2009

AOC CAHORS $12.95   245761

This is a very well-priced malbec from its French home in Cahors. It includes 20 percent merlot, which softens the texture somewhat and leads to a smooth yet edgy mouthfeel. The flavours are quite intense, nicely complex and layered, and the tannins are supple and quite manageable. Drink this with grilled red meats and well-seasoned, rich pastas and full-flavour cheeses.

NOTES

....

....

....

....

★ ★ ★ ★

Rigal 'The Original' Malbec 2010

AOC CAHORS $10.95   159178

L'Empire fights back! The success of malbec in Argentina seems to have prompted this producer to remind us that Cahors, in southwest France, is the original home of the variety. He or she points out that Argentinian and French malbec wines cannot be compared. Try it yourself with this restrained, concentrated and nicely balanced malbec. Try it with red meats or hearty stews . . . or with an Argentinian malbec.

NOTES

....

....

....

....

GERMANY

GERMANY IS FAR BETTER KNOWN for white wine than red, but it actually produces reds in many of its regions, and pinot noir is becoming an important variety. Because of the cool climate and relatively short growing season, they tend to be in a lighter and crisper style.

Important terms on German wine labels are *Prädikatswein* (the highest quality classification of wine) and *Qualitätswein* (known fully as *Qualitätswein bestimmter Anbaugebiete* [QbA]), which are designated as wines of quality but not of the highest level. *Landwein* indicates that the wine is made from grapes sourced from a broader region than the other classifications. Each of these terms is followed by the name of the wine region where the grapes were grown.

NEW!
★ ★ ★ ½

Baden Dry Pinot Noir 2010

QUALITÄTSWEIN BADEN $9.95   231373

Baden is the centre of pinot noir production in Germany. This one is dry and medium bodied, and straightforward and uncomplicated. The flavours are solid right through the palate and show decent complexity. They're supported by vibrant acidity that translates as a juicy texture, and it goes well with roasted and grilled poultry or pork, tomato-based casseroles and grilled salmon.

NOTES

....
....
....
....

NEW!
★ ★ ★ ★

Villa Wolf Pinot Noir 2009

QUALITÄTSWEIN PFALZ $14.95   291791

Made in a lighter-bodied and dry style, this pinot noir goes well with grilled or roasted poultry, roasted pork and grilled salmon. It will also pair nicely with many summer salads. The flavours are understated, solid right through the palate and nicely layered, and they are complemented by bright, pleasant acidity.

NOTES

....
....
....
....

GREECE

THE HOT GROWING CONDITIONS IN GREECE make for full-flavoured reds. Although many are produced from native grape varieties, notably agiorgitiko (sometimes called St. George), international varieties such as cabernet sauvignon are also making headway. An AOC-designated wine from Greece means that it complies with the laws regulating wine quality.

Hatzimichalis Cabernet Sauvignon 2006

★ ★ ★ ★

REGIONAL WINE OF ATALANTI VALLEY $17.95   638074

This is a quite powerful and very attractive cabernet sauvignon made in an international style. Look for flavours that are bold and intense, and echoed in the big, mouth-filling texture. This is a full-bodied cabernet that's dry and still quite tannic, and has a good seam of acidity that suits it for food. Serve it with grilled red meats, like lamb or beef, cooked medium rare at most and served with lemon wedges.

NOTES

....

....

....

....

ITALY

ITALY HAS LONG PRODUCED RED WINES from native grape varieties, but in recent years international varieties like merlot and cabernet sauvignon have also been planted. There are many regional varieties, the best-known being sangiovese, originally from Tuscany and now grown and used in winemaking throughout Italy. Other important varieties are nero d'Avola from Sicily and primitivo from southern Italy.

The highest-quality classification of Italian wines is DOCG (*Denominazione di Origine Controllata e Garantita*), indicating a wine made to stringent regulations and from a few specified grape varieties. Wines in the next category, DOC (*Denominazione di Origine Controllata*), follow similar rules. Wines labelled IGT (*Indicazione Geografica Tipica*) or IGP (*Indicazione Geografica Protetta*) are made according to less stringent regulations and may use a wider range of grape varieties. This doesn't mean that a DOCG wine is necessarily better than an IGT/IGP—in fact, some of Italy's most famous wines are IGT/IGP wines. Overall, you'll find quality and value in all these categories, as this list shows.

Allegrini 'Corte Giara' Ripasso Valpolicella 2009

DOC RIPASSO VALPOLICELLA $16.95 266692

Ripasso wines gain extra intensity from a second fermentation on the skins of partially dried grapes that were used in the production of amarone, the hefty Italian red. This ripasso delivers as it should, with quite plush, concentrated and layered flavours that are reined in by the bright, vibrant acidity. The tannins are moderate and drying, and this is a great bet for grilled red meats and braised ribs.

NOTES

Allegrini Valpolicella 2010

DOC VALPOLICELLA $13.95 230789

There are lots of valpolicellas on the market, and they range from the mediocre to the sublime. This one is definitely a cut above most. Here you'll find well-calibrated fruit that shows complexity and focus, partnered with a seam of fresh acidity that gives the wine a juicy texture. With moderate tannins, this goes well with a wide range of meat and vegetarian pasta dishes, and with meats like poultry, pork and veal.

NOTES

Ascheri Barbera d'Alba 2008

DOC BARBERA D'ALBA $13.95 219790

Barbera d'Alba is a too-little-known grape variety. Taste this lovely wine and you'll find that it delivers high-toned and concentrated flavours from start to finish, with a well-tuned texture that's fresh and lively. It's dry with light tannins, and it makes a great partner for many tomato-based Italian dishes (pizza, pasta, meats), as well as for pork, chicken and turkey dishes.

NOTES

Batasiolo Barolo 2007

★ ★ ★ ★ ½

DOCG BAROLO $26.75 178541

Barolo is considered one of Italy's great wines. Made from the nebbiolo variety in Piedmont, it's typically big, intense and very smooth. This one fits the description very well. You'll find real flavour intensity, with layered complexity and structure, together with a texture that's a tense combination of plush and fresh. The tannins are supple, and it's ready for grilled or roasted red meats and game.

NOTES

....
....
....
....

Bersano 'Costalunga' Barbera d'Asti 2010

★ ★ ★ ★

DOCG BARBERA D'ASTI $11.95 348680

Made from 100 percent barbera grapes, this is a widely versatile wine around food. Try it with burgers and pizza, red meats and poultry, pasta dishes and pork. Barbera is often like that when it's made in this style: dry and medium bodied, with solid and concentrated fruit, but understated rather than forward, with good balancing acidity and moderate tannins.

NOTES

....
....
....
....
....

NEW!
★ ★ ★ ½

Bolla Valpolicella Classico 2011

DOC VALPOLICELLA CLASSICO $11.95 16840

Valpolicella is a wine region in Veneto, in northeastern Italy, and all valpolicella wines are red. The most common grape is corvina, an Italian variety, and here it makes for a straightforward and very drinkable wine that's excellent for tomato-based pasta, meat and vegetable dishes. Look for well-focused fruit flavours and a juicy texture from the supporting acidity.

NOTES

....
....
....
....

Campo Maccione Morellino di Scansano 2009

NEW!
★★★ ½

DOCG MORELLINO DI SCANSANO $12.95   253831

From a small appellation in Tuscany, this is an attractive blend of sangiovese (known as morellino in the area), along with cabernet, merlot and syrah. It has a very fresh and vibrant texture, and the flavours are equally lively. It's dry, with negligible tannins, and is very versatile with food. Try it with tomato-based fish stews, chicken, pork and (of course) many Italian dishes.

NOTES

....

....

....

....

Carione Brunello di Montalcino 2005

NEW!
★★★★ ½

DOCG BRUNELLO DI MONTALCINO $29.95   266668

This is a very stylish red and a rare brunello (a clone of sangiovese grown in the Montalcino region) that's available year-round in Ontario. Look for elegance here, and a texture that's generous and smooth, yet high toned. The flavours are focused and subtly layered, and the tannins are present and supple. Well integrated, it goes well with red meats and full-flavoured Italian dishes.

NOTES

....

....

....

....

Casal Thaulero Sangiovese 2010

★★★★

IGT TERRE DI CHIETI $6.80   688996

This is a very attractive sangiovese. It has all the character you want from the grape—refreshing texture and fresh fruit flavour—and a bit more depth and complexity than most others around this low, low price. Look for bright flavours, a juicy texture and medium body. It's dry with light tannins, and it goes well with spaghetti bolognese, vegetarian lasagna and many pizzas.

NOTES

....

....

....

....

NEW!
★ ★ ★ ★ ½
CastelGiocondo Brunello di Montalcino 2006
DOCG BRUNELLO DI MONTALCINO $49.95   650432

[Vintages Essential] This beautiful red is made from sangiovese grapes and aged in barrels for three years. You'll find that the flavours are dense, deep and broad, with multi-layered complexity and firm tannins. All this is supported by a solid platform of acidity that cuts through the weight of the fruit, and makes for a tangy, fresh texture that invites you back to the glass. This is a big wine for big, well-seasoned food.

NOTES

....

....

....

....

NEW!
★ ★ ★ ½
Castellare Chianti Classico 2009
DOCG CHIANTI CLASSICO $18.95   267260

This is an organic wine from the original heart of the Chianti region (which is what the 'Classico' designation means). Mostly sangiovese, it shows concentrated fruit flavours that are brought to life by a lovely seam of bright acidity, resulting in an attractive juicy texture. It's dry, lightly tannic and medium bodied, and it goes well with tomato-based dishes, as well as with poultry and pork.

NOTES
....

....

....

....

★ ★ ★ ★
Cent'Are Nero d'Avola 2009
IGP SICILIA $13.95   646192

[Vintages Essential] The nero d'Avola (black grape of Avola) variety is native to Sicily and makes wines with intense flavours and colour. Cent'Are has been a popular Vintages Essential wine for years. It has concentrated flavours and moderate tannins, and is dry and medium bodied. Drink this with tasty vegetarian dishes like portobello burgers or with red meats.

NOTES
....

....

....

Cesari Amarone Classico 2007

★ ★ ★ ★ ½

DOC AMARONE DELLA VALPOLICELLA CLASSICO

$36.00   426718

This has the structure and concentration of flavours expected from a well-made amarone. It's deep and broad, with layers of pungent, vibrant and mature flavours that come on in waves. The texture is rich, tangy, mouth filling and surprisingly lively, given the weight of the wine. Dry, full bodied and delicious, this amarone calls for substantial and well-seasoned red meat dishes, like a rosemary/garlic rack of lamb or pepper steak.

NOTES

....

....

....

Cesari 'Mara' Valpolicella Superiore Ripasso 2009

★ ★ ★ ★

DOC VALPOLICELLA SUPERIORE $15.95   606519

This is a big, dense red with a plush and smooth texture that's a good choice when you're grilling red meats, game or richly flavoured sausages. It has attractive and full-flavoured fruit and good complexity. The tannins are moderate and drying, and, although it's lower in acidity than you might expect, there's some distinct juiciness to the texture.

NOTES

....

....

....

....

....

Citra Montepulciano d'Abruzzo 2010

★ ★ ★ ★

DOC MONTEPULCIANO D'ABRUZZO $6.95   446633

Like many Italian wine names, this combines a grape variety (montepulciano) and a wine region (Abruzzo). This is a surprisingly well-made wine for the price. You get rich, concentrated flavours that flow through from start to finish. It might not be all that complex, but the texture is very attractive—tangy and refreshing—and ideal for grilled red meats and hearty tomato-based vegetarian stews.

NOTES

....

....

....

....

NEW!
★ ★ ★ ½

Concilio Pinot Noir 2008

IGT VIGNETI DELLE DOLOMITI $11.95 257030

Italy is not the first place you would go to find pinot noir, but it's planted there. This example is a lighter-bodied style, with understated and attractive flavours supported by a good seam of fresh, clean acidity. It's dry and barely tannic, and goes well with roasted or grilled poultry and salmon.

NOTES

....

....

....

....

....

★ ★ ★ ★

Cusumano Nero d'Avola 2010

IGT SICILIA $9.95 143164

Sicily is coming to the fore with some high-quality and many good value wines. This is one of the latter, made from the indigenous variety that's become the island's signature grape. Here you get quite intense flavours with limited complexity and good consistency, and an attractive tangy texture. With moderate tannins, it's a good bet for well-flavoured red meats and pasta dishes.

NOTES

....

....

....

....

NEW!
★ ★ ★ ★

Enzo Vincenzo Valpolicella Ripasso 2009

DOC VALPOLICELLA RIPASSO $14.05 194118

Look for quite intense flavours, with layers of complexity, partly derived from fermenting on the skins of grapes used for making rich amarone. There's good acidity here, and a tangy, juicy texture framed by ripe, moderate tannins. Dry and a bit more than medium in body, it's great with red meats, as well as hearty pastas, stews and risottos.

NOTES

....

....

....

....

Farina 'Le Pezze' Ripasso Valpolicella Classico Superiore 2007

DOC VALPOLICELLA CLASSICO SUPERIORE $13.80 195966

The name is quite a mouthful, but then, so is the wine. The flavours are rich and dense, with depth and complexity, and the texture is fleshy and generous. The acidity provides a nice counterbalance, weighing in with life and freshness, and the tannins are moderate. This is a very good wine to go with steak Florentine, and with red meats and rich pastas in general.

NOTES

....

....

....

....

★ ★ ★ ★ ½

Farnese 'Casale Vecchio' Montepulciano d'Abruzzo 2010

DOC MONTEPULCIANO D'ABRUZZO $9.90 612788

This is a very impressive wine, with flavours that are sweet, rich and dense but well defined, and good complexity. It's dense and mouth filling in texture, but the acidity is well integrated and leaves your palate feeling saturated but refreshed. Dry and full bodied, it's a great choice for meat-rich Italian dishes and for any red meat and hearty stew.

NOTES

....

....

....

....

....

★ ★ ★ ★

Farnese Negroamaro 2010

IGT PUGLIA $7.85 143735

Negroamaro ("black bitter") is a variety indigenous to the south of Italy, where this wine comes from. Despite the name, this wine is deep red (not black) and full of sweet and ripe (not bitter) flavours. It has very good acidity, is dry with easygoing tannins and is a great choice for casual meals of pasta, burgers and many red meats.

NOTES

....

....

....

....

....

Farnese Sangiovese 2007

★ ★ ★

IGT DAUNIA $7.45   612327

When this wine first hit the LCBO's shelves some years ago, its price/ quality combination made it an instant hit. It flew off the shelves, and the LCBO had trouble keeping it in stock. It's still very good value, even though it's climbed slightly in price. Look for bright and vibrant flavours, medium weight and a refreshing texture. You can't go wrong serving this with pizza and tomato sauce–based pasta.

NOTES

Folonari Valpolicella Classico 2010

NEW!
★ ★ ★ ★

DOC VALPOLICELLA CLASSICO $12.95   828

Folonari valpolicella has been around for years, and continues to offer good value for money. It has a high-toned feel to it, with bright but serious flavours and a juicy texture from the healthy dose of acidity underlying them. It's dry and medium bodied and goes well with Italian dishes, especially those with tomatoes or tomato sauce.

NOTES

Fontanafredda Barolo 2007

★ ★ ★ ★ ½

DOCG BAROLO $29.85   20214

This is a gorgeous wine, one of those winners that combines power and depth with elegance and style. The fruit flavours are concentrated and nicely structured, and they're complemented by refreshing and well-calibrated acidity. The tannins are firm and ripe, and the wine is a great choice if you're having osso bucco or any meat in a tomato-based sauce.

NOTES

Fontanafredda 'Briccotondo' Barbera 2010

★ ★ ★ ★ ½

DOC PIEMONTE $15.95   72348

Barbera is a variety that deserves to be more popular. Take this example, which delivers great flavours that are layered and serious, but fresh and vibrant. The acidity is pitched right—forward and juicy but not at all harsh—and the tannins are drying but in the background. It's a perfect wine for mushroom risotto or for any tomato-based Italian dish.

NOTES
....
....
....
....
....

Gabbiano Chianti 2010

★ ★ ★ ★

DOCG CHIANTI $13.95   78006

The grapes for this dry, medium-weight wine are from the estate of the Castello di Gabbiano, a thirteenth-century castle located on a hill in chianti classico country. In the bottle you'll find attractive flavours that are solid, fresh and concentrated, with good complexity. They're complemented by a tangy and refreshing texture and great balance. This goes very well with a rich, tomato-based pasta, or any stew in a red wine and tomato sauce.

NOTES
....
....
....
....

Gabbiano Chianti Classico 2008

NEW!
★ ★ ★ ★ ★

DOCG CHIANTI CLASSICO $16.95   219808

'Classico' means that the grapes for the wine came from the area that was originally demarcated for chianti; it has been expanded over time. This example delivers lovely rich and focused flavours with impressive complexity and range. They're complemented and supported by fresh acidity that gives a sleek and refreshing texture, and are framed by supple tannins. Drink it with classic Italian dishes.

NOTES
....
....
....

NEW!
★ ★ ★ ★

Illuminati Riparosso Montepulciano d'Abruzzo 2009

DOC MONTEPULCIANO D'ABRUZZO $12.95   269985

Montepulciano is the grape variety and Abruzzo is the region. They work beautifully together to make wines like this, with rich, concentrated flavours, nice complexity and very good fruit-acid balance, leading to a high-toned, tangy texture. This is a versatile red that's great with hearty Italian dishes (lasagna, osso bucco), with red meats generally and even with pork.

NOTES
....
....
....
....

NEW!
★ ★ ★ ★ ½

Luccarelli Primitivo 2010

IGP PUGLIA $9.70   253856

Less expensive primitivo—the variety now associated with the southern region of Puglia—can be intense and heavy. This one achieves real lightness of being, and brings a juicy texture without sacrificing the concentration of flavour. It's a very attractive and, more importantly, very drinkable wine, and goes well with many tomato-based dishes, as well as poultry and pork.

NOTES
....
....
....
....
....

NEW!
★ ★ ★ ★

Masi 'Bonacosta' Valpolicella Classico 2010

DOC VALPOLICELLA CLASSICO $14.95   285583

Made from the classic varieties (corvina, rondinella, molinara) in the original (classico) area of Valpolicella, this is a lovely red that goes beautifully with steak Florentine, hearty pastas and red meats generally. The flavours are deep and broad, with complexity and focus, and the texture is full, sleek and, above all, refreshing.

NOTES
....
....
....
....

Masi Campofiorin 2008

★★★★ ½

IGT ROSSO DEL VERONESE $17.95   155051

Campofiorin is a stylish wine that's reliable year after year. It's made by adding freshly fermented wine to the grape skins that remain after the super-rich amarone is made. The result has dense, intense flavours of complex, ripe fruit. It's more than medium bodied, and dry with a tangy texture. It's a real treat to drink, and goes well with spicy pasta dishes with grated Parmigiano Reggiano.

NOTES

....

....

....

....

Masi 'Costasera' Amarone della Valpolicella Classico 2007

★★★★ ½

DOC AMARONE DELLA VALPOLICELLA CLASSICO

$39.95   317057

Amarone is made from grapes that are allowed to dry on bamboo mats for a few months before being pressed. The drying process leads to more concentrated flavours and complexity, as this wine shows. Its layers of ripe and mature fruit are dense and well focused, and it has an opulent texture. Dry and moderately tannic with a tangy texture, it's an excellent choice for rich red meat dishes and aged hard cheeses.

NOTES

....

....

....

....

Masi Modello delle Venezie 2010

NEW!
★★★★ ½

IGT ROSSO DELLE VENEZIE $19.95   27854

It's just a very well-made wine, sourced from the grape varieties common in the Veneto region. The flavours are full and generous, but nicely complex and layered, and they're lifted by a lovely seam of refreshing acidity. It's dry, smooth and medium bodied, and just perfect with red meats and hearty pastas.

NOTES

....

....

....

....

NEW!
★ ★ ★ ½

Matervitae Negroamaro 2008

IGT PUGLIA $9.50 254300

This is another of the many inexpensive Italian wines that offer good value. From the southern region of Puglia, and made from a grape that translates as "bitter black," this offers edgy (but not bitter) and concentrated flavours and a really tangy texture. It's dry with moderate tannins, and it's a great buy for burgers, grilled red meats and the like.

NOTES

....
....
....
....
....

NEW!
★ ★ ★ ½

Mezzomondo Negroamaro 2010

IGT SALENTO $7.90 688962

This red, from the south of Italy, is an example of the good value available at lower price points. It offers plenty of flavour, with some complexity and depth. Toss in a good dose of acidity and you have the texture you need for food, like many tomato-based pasta, meat and vegetable dishes. It's dry, medium bodied and lightly tannic.

NOTES

....
....
....
....
....

★ ★ ★ ★ ½

Montalto Nero d'Avola/Cabernet Sauvignon 2010

IGT SICILIA $8.95 621151

For a long time, Sicily was better known for white wine than red, but in the last few years the reds, led by the native nero d'Avola grape variety, have been going gangbusters. Nero d'Avola is most of the blend here, and it delivers rich, complex flavours of dark fruit and spice. It's almost full bodied, with a generous and tangy texture. This is fairly big and needs the same kind of food, so pair it with well-seasoned red meat.

NOTES

....
....
....
....

Monte Antico 2007

IGT TOSCANA $15.95   69377

[Vintages Essential] This delicious wine is a blend of sangiovese, the
signature red grape variety of Italy, and merlot and cabernet sauvignon.
It delivers robust and concentrated flavours that display complexity
and depth, and a plush, full texture that's refreshing and tangy. A hint
of rusticity adds to its attractiveness. This is an excellent wine for full-
bodied Italian dishes, and it extends equally well to other rich meat and
vegetarian cuisines.

NOTES

Negrar Amarone della Valpolicella Classico 2008

★ ★ ★ ★ ½

DOC AMARONE DELLA VALPOLICELLA CLASSICO

$34.95   44784

Plush, mouth filling and richly textured, this is a lovely amarone that
delivers firm tannins and layers of concentrated flavour. It has just the
right acidity needed to contain the richness of the fruit and make for
a wine that pairs successfully with food. Enjoy this with any meal that
features well-seasoned red meats. Alternatively, drink it with aged hard
cheese such as Parmigiano Reggiano.

NOTES

Negrar Valpolicella Classico 2010

NEW!
★ ★ ★ ★

DOC VALPOLICELLA CLASSICO $12.95   8334

This is a medium-bodied red on the lighter end of the spectrum, from the
original Valpolicella region in northern Italy. The fruit is ripe and nicely
concentrated without being dense, and the acidity gives the wine a juicy
texture that makes you want another sip . . . another glass. It's a natural
for much Italian cuisine, but also goes well with chicken, grilled salmon
and roasted pork.

NOTES

Nipozzano Riserva Chianti Rufina 2008

★ ★ ★ ★

DOC CHIANTI RUFINA $21.95   107276

If you're looking for a red wine to go with your lasagna, veal scaloppini or other Italian food, try this. But it also goes well with poultry, pork and many red meats, and vegetable dishes not prepared in an Italian style. Open this bottle to discover concentrated flavours, easygoing tannins and a texture that's fresh and bright. It's dry and medium bodied and really sings when it's introduced to food.

NOTES

....

....

....

....

Rocca delle Macìe Chianti Classico 2009

★ ★ ★ ★

DOCG CHIANTI CLASSICO $18.95   741769

[Vintages Essential] This is a long-time favourite chianti classico (the "classico" meaning the grapes came from the original Chianti region, which has been expanded over time). It's a quite young chianti, with bright and vibrant flavours and a lively texture. Dry and medium bodied, it goes well with Italian tomato-based dishes, whether pasta, meat or pizza.

NOTES

....

....

....

....

....

Rocca delle Macìe 'Vernaiolo' Chianti 2010

★ ★ ★ ★

DOCG CHIANTI $19.95   269589

The Chianti wine region produces tens of millions of bottles of wine a year, some of it exquisite, some of it not. If you're old enough to have been drinking chianti in the 1960s and 1970s, you'll remember some of the not-exquisite chiantis in wicker baskets. Luckily, Vernaiolo is an attractive chianti with quite concentrated flavours of ripe fruit. It's dry and moderately tannic, juicy textured and perfect with chicken parmesan.

NOTES

....

....

....

....

Secco-Bertani Ripasso Valpolicella-Valpantena 2009

NEW!
★ ★ ★ ★

DOC VALPOLICELLA-VALPANTENA $15.50   12443

Valpolicella is a wine region in northeast Italy where the wines are made mainly from the corvina grape variety. This example is a full-bodied red with plenty of complexity and richness, partly from the dried skins used during fermentation. The acidity comes through nicely, showing as a refreshing texture verging on juicy, and the tannins are manageable. Drink this with rich pasta dishes, red meats and full-flavoured cheeses.

NOTES

Sella & Mosca Cannonau di Sardegna Riserva 2008

NEW!
★ ★ ★ ★ ½

DOC CANNONAU DI SARDEGNA $15.95   425488

[Vintages Essential] Grape varieties have different names in different regions, and cannonau is more commonly known as grenache or, in Spain, garnacha. This example from Sardinia has some interesting and rustic qualities, and it goes really well with grilled red meats and burgers. It's full bodied, with dense and intense flavours, and has a very tangy texture from the balancing acidity.

NOTES

Serego Alighieri 'Poderi del Bello Ovile' Toscana 2008

NEW!
★ ★ ★ ★ ½

IGT TOSCANA $15.45   73106

This is a delicious blend of sangiovese, canaiolo and ciliegiolo varieties. Their merger has resulted in a full-bodied, plush, textured wine that delivers intense, layered and focused flavours. The tannins are moderate. This is a wine that goes well with well-seasoned or richly flavoured food like game, grilled red meats and hearty pasta dishes.

NOTES

Serego Alighieri 'Possessioni Rosso' 2009

NEW!
★★★★

IGT ROSSO DEL VERONESE $14.95   447326

Masi is a well-known producer of quality wines, and this delicious red blend (mainly corvina and sangiovese grape varieties) shows the value it offers, too. This has concentrated and nicely nuanced flavours, and you'll find the texture attractive and juicy. Medium bodied and dry, it's a natural candidate for Italian dishes, from vegetarian pizza to veal scaloppini.

NOTES
....
....
....
....
....

Stlto Malbec/Merlot 2010

NEW!
★★★ ½

ITALY $11.95   232272

The grapes for this wine were grown in the Abruzzo region, in central Italy. It's mostly (80 percent) malbec, and delivers a lot of flavour and intensity. The acid-fruit balance is good (making for a fairly fresh texture) and it's dry with easygoing tannins. It's a versatile wine for food: Think of it for burgers, poultry, pork and fairly simple red meat dishes.

NOTES
....
....
....
....

Tedeschi Amarone della Valpolicella Classico 2007

★★★★ ½

DOC AMARONE DELLA VALPOLICELLA CLASSICO

$36.95   433417

[Vintages Essential] The grapes for this wine are dried for four months, allowing them to shrivel and the water in them to evaporate. When they're finally pressed they have more concentrated flavours. The wine is then aged for two to three years in oak barrels and another six months in the bottle. Taste the process in the rich, intense, complex flavours and the almost decadently opulent texture. This needs big, rich food, such as lamb, steak or game.

NOTES
....
....
....

NEW!
★★★★

Terre del Barolo 'Vinum Vita Est' Barolo 2006

DOCG BAROLO $24.80   264333

The Latin translates as "wine is life," which might be true for some of us. But even if your life extends beyond wine, you'll find this one a great partner for heavier, full-flavoured dishes, like grilled or roasted game, and well-seasoned beef and lamb. The flavours here are dense and deep, with loads of complexity and supple tannins. There's also a good dose of acidity to keep everything under control.

NOTES
....
....
....
....

NEW!
★★★ ½

Tini Sangiovese di Romagna 2010

DOC SANGIOVESE DI ROMAGNA $8.75   179432

At this price, you can't go wrong with this wine when you're hosting friends for pizza or pasta. Made from sangiovese in the region of Romagna, it's a dry red with a texture that's concentrated and bright. The freshness of the acidity shows through nicely and complements the vibrant flavours, which are modestly complex but consistent from start to finish.

NOTES
....
....
....
....

NEW!
★★★★★

Umberto Fiore Barbaresco 2006

DOCG BARBARESCO $16.50   254870

Made from nebbiolo grapes in an appellation near Barbaresco in the region of Piedmont, this is a beautiful wine with poise and style. Already more than six years old, it shows maturing fruit flavours that are still lively and fresh, with vibrant acidity and drying tannins. It's medium bodied and a perfect choice for roasted poultry, grilled duck and many medium- to strong-flavoured mature cheeses.

NOTES
....
....
....
....
....

NEW!
★ ★ ★ ★

Velletri 'Terre dei Volsci' Riserva 2007

DOC VELLETRI $14.05   175141

Don't panic, that *is* a weirdly shaped bottle—not the aftershock of the
16 percent zinfandel you drank last night. Velletri is a region in Lazio,
south of Tuscany, and the reds from there are mostly montepulciano and
sangiovese. This delivers a lovely smooth and tangy texture (sounds odd,
but try it), with vibrant and focused flavours. Dry and medium bodied,
it's excellent with rich tomato-based pastas and pizzas.

NOTES
....
....
....
....

NEW!
★ ★ ★ ★ ½

Zenato Ripassa Valpolicella Superiore 2008

DOC VALPOLICELLA SUPERIORE RIPASSO $24.95   479766

[Vintages Essential] Ripasso wine is made by fermenting it on the skins
of grapes that have been used for making amarone. They give ripassos
richness and complexity, as this one shows so well. The flavours are deep
and broad, layered and solid, and they're complemented by clean acidity
that translates as a tangy texture. It's a great choice for steaks, red meat
roasts and full-flavoured aged cheeses.

NOTES
....
....
....
....

NEW!
★ ★ ★ ★

Zenato Veneto Rosso 2009

IGT VENETO $11.45   208579

This red brings two international varieties, cabernet sauvignon and merlot,
into a partnership with corvina, a variety native to Veneto, in northeastern
Italy. The combination leads to flavours that are concentrated and
consistent, and the corvina adds some fresh acidity that lifts everything
and orients the wine to food. Drink it with red meats, pork and poultry
and with hearty, tomato-based vegetable ragouts.

NOTES
....
....
....
....

NEW ZEALAND

NEW ZEALAND IS BEST KNOWN for its white wine, especially sauvignon blancs from the Marlborough region in the South Island. But it turns out many very good red wines, too, including merlots from the North Island. The pinot noirs are especially impressive, notably those from Central Otago (the world's southernmost wine region) and Marlborough, two regions in the South Island. Most are made in volumes too small for the LCBO General Purchase list, but we are seeing a better selection every year.

★ ★ ★ ★ ½

Kim Crawford Pinot Noir 2010

MARLBOROUGH $19.95 626390

[Vintages Essential] Kim Crawford is one of New Zealand's best-known winemakers, and here he lends his name to a very attractive pinot noir. From grapes grown in the very sunny but cool Marlborough wine region, it shows lovely focused and layered flavours that are harnessed to fresh acidity and framed by supple tannins. It's quite delicious and a great partner for roasted or grilled lamb.

NOTES

NEW!
★ ★ ★ ★

Mud House Pinot Noir 2009

CENTRAL OTAGO $17.95 190462

Central Otago, in the south of the South Island, is the southernmost wine region in the world, and it has quickly gained a reputation for its fine pinot noirs. This well-priced example shows lovely fruit that's concentrated and layered, paired with a broad seam of fresh acidity. Dry and moderately tannic, this tangy red goes well with roasted red meats, duck breast and mushroom risotto.

NOTES

NEW!
★ ★ ★ ★

The People's Pinot Noir 2010

CENTRAL OTAGO $16.95 234526

With its funky label, off-the-wall name and suggestion you pair it with "film, fire and friends," your expectations of this wine might be low. In fact, it's a well-made pinot with good complexity and breadth in the ripe flavours, a fresh, juicy texture and supple, if modest, tannins. It's a good partner for grilled salmon and roasted chicken and turkey.

NOTES

Stoneleigh Pinot Noir 2010

★ ★ ★ ★

MARLBOROUGH $19.95   64353

Marlborough is best known for the sauvignon blancs that stormed world markets in the 1990s, but in terms of varieties planted, it's quite diverse. This lovely pinot noir shows the region's versatility. It delivers quite pure fruit flavours that are complex and layered, and a lovely, rich, tangy texture that's great for food. This pinot will go well with duck breast, grilled salmon, roasted turkey and even roasted lamb.

NOTES

....

....

....

....

Villa Maria 'Private Bin' Pinot Noir 2009

★ ★ ★ ★

MARLBOROUGH $19.95   268417

Pinot noir is a popular wine partly because it's versatile with food. Depending on style, it goes well with red meats, poultry, pork, many vegetarian dishes and some fish and seafood. This example shows intense flavours with some sweet notes, good complexity and the right acidity to make it juicy. Try it with roasted duck or turkey, grilled salmon or mushroom risotto.

NOTES

....

....

....

....

Whitehaven Pinot Noir 2009

NEW!
★ ★ ★ ★ ½

MARLBOROUGH $22.95   245696

This is a delicious pinot noir that carries all the hallmarks of the common New Zealand style: plenty of concentrated fruit, with layers of complexity and rich, yet understated flavour, harnessed to bright, vibrant acidity. Dry and more than medium in body, this has more power than many in the LCBO, and it goes well with rich poultry and pork dishes, and easily stretches to roasted red meats.

NOTES

....

....

....

....

ONTARIO

THE MOST SUCCESSFUL RED GRAPE VARIETIES in Ontario are those that regularly thrive and ripen in its cool climate. They include gamay, pinot noir and cabernet franc. The best-known of Ontario's four wine regions is Niagara Peninsula (which is now divided into a number of sub-regions). Lake Erie North Shore, which is somewhat warmer, is also represented in this list.

Wine labelled VQA (Vintners Quality Alliance) followed by a region is made from grapes grown in that region. The VQA classification also means that the wine has been tested and tasted. VQA wines from Ontario can be made only from grapes grown in Ontario.

Most non-VQA wines in the Ontario section of the LCBO are blends of a small proportion of Ontario wine and foreign wine. They are not included in this book because the range varies greatly from year to year, depending on the Ontario grape harvest.

Cave Spring Cellars Gamay 2010

★ ★ ★ ★

VQA NIAGARA PENINSULA $14.95   228569

Gamay grapes grow very successfully in the Niagara Peninsula, but it's a variety overlooked by too many wine drinkers. This one from Cave Spring is lovely. It has bright flavours of fresh fruit and a refreshing texture. It's dry and light-to-medium bodied, and the juiciness in the texture makes you think of food. Drink it with roasted chicken or baked ham. I like to serve it just slightly chilled.

NOTES

....

....

....

....

Cave Spring Cellars Pinot Noir 2010

NEW!
★ ★ ★ ★

VQA NIAGARA PENINSULA $17.95   417642

Cave Spring built its reputation on riesling, but it fires on all varietal cylinders. For example, this is a really fine-tasting pinot noir. Look for vibrant fruit with good complexity, a slightly tangy and very refreshing texture, and drying tannins that are easily handled. It's dry and medium bodied, and a nice match for roasted turkey or chicken, poached salmon or a tomato-based vegetarian dish.

NOTES

....

....

....

....

Château des Charmes Gamay Noir 2009

★ ★ ★ ★

VQA NIAGARA-ON-THE-LAKE $12.55   67349

Gamay is the grape variety used to make beaujolais, but this wine is more substantial than most generic beaujolais, and is another wine that makes the case that gamay should be Ontario's red grape variety. What you get is concentrated flavours and a generous texture that's food-friendly and refreshing. It's medium bodied and dry, and goes really well with roast turkey and cranberries, chicken, pork and many pastas.

NOTES

....

....

....

....

Château des Charmes Pinot Noir 2007

★ ★ ★ ★ ½

VQA NIAGARA-ON-THE-LAKE $14.55 195511

This is a really lovely bone dry, medium-bodied pinot noir that makes a great choice when you're serving dishes such as well-seasoned lamb, grilled duck breast or rich mushroom risotto. The fruit is ripe and solid right through the palate, with excellent complexity and concentration, and it's combined with fresh acidity—which shows as juiciness—and moderate tannins.

NOTES

....

....

....

....

Coyote's Run Cabernet/Merlot 2010

★ ★ ★ ★

VQA NIAGARA PENINSULA $16.50 26757

This blend (of cabernet franc, cabernet sauvignon and merlot) delivers very attractive and well-extracted flavours. Dry and medium bodied, it shows a generous and almost fleshy texture, with tannins that grip gently and with suppleness. It's a very good choice for roasted, grilled or braised red meats, and it also goes with pork, chicken and aged cheeses.

NOTES

....

....

....

....

Coyote's Run Five Mile Red 2010

NEW!
★ ★ ★ ½

VQA NIAGARA PENINSULA $16.95 283416

This blend of pinot noir, merlot, syrah and cabernet franc is attractive, easy drinking and very versatile with food. It's medium weight and dry with light tannins, and the flavours are solid all the way through. With the acidity contributing an almost juicy texture, this goes well with turkey, chicken and pork, but it also extends to roasted or grilled red meats.

NOTES

....

....

....

....

Dan Aykroyd 'Discovery Series' Merlot 2007

NEW!
★★★★

VQA ONTARIO $14.95   214940

What struck me first about this merlot was its juicy texture, making it
the style of wine that goes so well with food. And this is an easy choice
not only for red meats, but also hearty pasta, roast pork and even poultry.
It shows layered, ripe fruit flavours, and good integration of the oak and
tannins. Overall, it performs very successfully—like its namesake.

NOTES

....

....

....

....

....

Fielding Estate Red Conception 2009

NEW!
★★★ ½

VQA NIAGARA PENINSULA $18.95   189183

A blend of merlot, cabernet sauvignon and syrah, this is dry and on the
lighter side of medium bodied. It shows understated flavours with subtle
hints of oak, and a fairly tangy, crisp texture. It doesn't have the heft for
richer red meats, so pair it with roasted chicken or turkey, grilled salmon
or many tomato-based pasta dishes.

NOTES

....

....

....

....

Flat Rock Pinot Noir 2010

NEW!
★★★★ ½

VQA NIAGARA ESCARPMENT $19.95   1545

[Vintages Essential] Flat Rock Cellars is named for the large flat rocks
discovered when the land was excavated to build the winery. This pinot
noir is representative of the winery's consistent quality: The fruit is
complex and well defined, and it's nicely harmonized with the clean, fresh
acidity that translates as a juicy texture. Medium bodied and dry, with
supple tannins, this stylish pinot is built for roasted poultry, mushroom
risotto and grilled salmon.

NOTES

....

....

....

....

Henry of Pelham Baco Noir 2010

★ ★ ★ ★

VQA ONTARIO $13.95   270926

A few wineries make successful wine from baco noir, a variety that's widely grown in Niagara. The characteristic flavours are a bit beyond the mainstream (it's sometimes described as "funky"), but it has a real following. Henry of Pelham is known as a producer that understands the variety, and in this example you'll find rich, pungent flavours with a lot of complexity. Dry, medium bodied and nicely balanced, it goes well with rich, well-seasoned red meat.

NOTES

....

....

....

Henry of Pelham Cabernet/Merlot 2010

★ ★ ★ ★

VQA NIAGARA PENINSULA $14.95   604241

Blends of cabernet (sometimes cabernet sauvignon, sometimes cabernet franc, sometimes both) with merlot are made everywhere, with varying success. This is a quite attractive example, with concentrated and well-defined flavours, moderately gripping tannins and a generous texture that's refreshing and friendly to food. Drink it with roast beef and root vegetables, or a hearty winter vegetarian stew.

NOTES

....

....

....

....

Henry of Pelham Pinot Noir 2009

★ ★ ★ ★

VQA NIAGARA PENINSULA $16.95   13904

Henry of Pelham is one of Niagara's mid-size, quality wineries, run by the affable Speck brothers (three of them). The wine is made by long-time partner Ron Giesbrecht. With great balance between the fruit and acidity, this attractive pinot noir makes a successful partner for grilled lamb, veal chops or well-herbed roast chicken. It's medium bodied, with attractive and vibrant flavours and a juicy, refreshing texture.

NOTES

....

....

....

NEW!
★ ★ ★ ½

Inniskillin Pinot Noir 2010

VQA NIAGARA PENINSULA $14.95   261099

It looks fairly light in the glass, and the weight is on the lighter side of medium, but this dry pinot noir delivers nicely concentrated flavours and decent complexity. They're enhanced by the underlying seam of acidity that comes through as juiciness in the texture, and the whole is framed by firm tannins. It's a very good choice for roasted or grilled poultry and pork.

NOTES

....

....

....

....

NEW!
★ ★ ★ ★

Jackson-Triggs 'Black Series' Cabernet Franc/Cabernet Sauvignon 2010

VQA NIAGARA PENINSULA $12.95   660680

These are two of the main red varieties of bordeaux, and here they make for a big-bodied and intensely flavoured red that's a very good choice for grilled red meats and other hearty dishes. The flavours are dense and complex, and the texture is very dry, but generous, full and juicy, with firm tannins.

NOTES

....

....

....

....

NEW!
★ ★ ★ ★

Jackson-Triggs 'Black Series' Merlot 2010

VQA NIAGARA PENINSULA $13.95   109959

This is a fairly attractive merlot that goes equally well with red meats and the more delicate flavours of roast chicken and pork. It's quite astringently dry and delivers nicely defined flavours right through the palate. There's refreshing acidity and good balance, as you expect from a cool-climate merlot, and overall it's a well-made wine that's very versatile on your dinner table.

NOTES

....

....

....

....

Kacaba Cabernet/Merlot 2009

NEW!
★ ★ ★ ½

VQA NIAGARA ESCARPMENT $16.95   101477

Kacaba (pronounced ka-SAH-ba) is a smaller Niagara winery that produces many quality wines. This one is mostly cabernet franc, with contributions from merlot and cabernet sauvignon. With a hint of herbaceousness from the franc or the vintage, the flavours are full and complex, the texture is edgily tangy and the tannins are firm. It's a very good choice for red meats (and an acidic condiment) and many rich pastas.

NOTES

Konzelmann Reserve Merlot 2009

NEW!
★ ★ ★ ★

VQA NIAGARA PENINSULA $12.95   439281

This is a very solid cool-climate merlot, different from merlot from warmer regions in that it offers more restrained flavour and a fruit-acid balance tuned to food. Look for good complexity here, with freshness and gentle but perceptible tannins. Dry and medium bodied, it goes well with roasted or grilled poultry, a veal chop and many meat- or vegetable-based stews.

NOTES

Megalomaniac 'Homegrown Cellar 4379' Red 2009

NEW!
★ ★ ★ ½

VQA NIAGARA PENINSULA $14.95   260364

This is a robust red blend. The fruit is concentrated and nicely layered, with a touch of attractive herbaceousness. The acidity is well calibrated, coming through as a refreshing texture, and the whole is bounded by firm tannins. It's dry and medium bodied, and you can confidently serve it with grilled or roasted red meats, as well as with hearty pastas and stews.

NOTES

NEW!
★ ★ ★ ½

Open Cab²-Merlot 2009

VQA NIAGARA PENINSULA $11.95   134957

The symbol isn't right: This is not the square of a cabernet, but two cabernets (franc and sauvignon), so it ought to be '2Cabs-Merlot.' Brand quibbles aside, it's a full-flavoured blend that makes a good choice for burgers, ribs and red meats, and also pork and some poultry dishes. Dry, medium bodied and fruity, it shows easygoing tannins.

NOTES

....

....

....

....

....

NEW!
★ ★ ★ ½

Peninsula Ridge Cabernet/Merlot 2010

VQA NIAGARA PENINSULA $14.95   70052

Cabernet sauvignon doesn't ripen well in all Niagara vintages, but as the dominant grape in this blend, it comes through well. The flavours are concentrated and have decent complexity, while the texture is tangy and verging on juicy. It's dry and medium weight and has moderate tannins. It makes a very good partner for red meats, burgers and hearty stews (meat and veggie).

NOTES

....

....

....

....

....

NEW!
★ ★ ★ ½

Peninsula Ridge Merlot 2010

VQA NIAGARA PENINSULA $14.95   61101

This is an attractive merlot that displays solid fruit flavours from start to finish. They're quite concentrated and complex, and complemented by a texture that's both generous and refreshing. It's dry and medium bodied with easygoing tannins, and a good bet for grilled or roasted red meats.

NOTES

....

....

....

....

....

NEW!
★ ★ ★ ½

Pillitteri Cabernet/Merlot 2010

VQA NIAGARA PENINSULA $12.95   349191

This is a blend of cabernets franc and sauvignon (45 percent each) and merlot. It shows well-concentrated and decently complex flavours that hold consistently from start to finish, with a texture that's round, smooth and verging on juicy. It's dry and medium bodied with easygoing tannins, and it goes well with a wide range of red meats, roasted poultry and pork.

NOTES

....

....

....

....

....

NEW!
★ ★ ★ ½

Red House Cabernet/Shiraz 2009

VQA NIAGARA PENINSULA $12.95   219030

Made by Henry of Pelham, this is a straightforward and well-made, medium-bodied red blend that goes well with red meats, burgers, ribs, pizza . . . you get the gastronomic picture. The fruit flavours are concentrated with decent complexity, the acidity contributes tanginess to the texture, it's dry, dry, dry and it has moderate tannins.

NOTES

....

....

....

....

....

NEW!
★ ★ ★ ½

Sandbanks Reserve Baco Noir 2009

VQA ONTARIO $19.95   225920

Sandbanks winery is located in Prince Edward County, close to the shore of Lake Ontario. (VQA rules specify that hybrid grape varieties, like baco noir, can only be labelled with the Ontario appellation.) This is a lovely wine that's rich in concentrated fruit, is a lot less funky than many bacos and has a generous and soft texture. It goes well with grilled or roasted red meats.

NOTES

....

....

....

NEW!
★ ★ ★ ★ ½

Southbrook Connect Red 2011

VQA NIAGARA-ON-THE-LAKE $14.95   249565

This is a very well-made red from one of Niagara's more stunning wineries. It's organic and made from roughly equal parts of cabernets franc and sauvignon and merlot. Look for a lovely, soft but refreshing texture supporting fruit that's ripe, focused and quite complex. It's dry, with fairly firm tannins, and goes well with red meats, pork and hearty vegetarian dishes.

NOTES

....

....

....

....

NEW!
★ ★ ★ ★

Sprucewood Shores Lady in Red 2010

VQA LAKE ERIE NORTH SHORE $14.95   266486

Sprucewood Shores winery is actually on the shore of Lake Erie. This is a really lovely blend of merlot, cabernet sauvignon and cabernet franc that shows consistency from start to finish and good complexity. The acidity is very well balanced and contributes freshness and juiciness to the texture. Dry, with supple tannins, it's a very good choice for grilled and roasted red meats, pork and many hearty poultry dishes.

NOTES

....

....

....

....

NEW!
★ ★ ★ ★

Stoney Ridge Pinot Noir 2010

VQA NIAGARA PENINSULA $13.95   156125

It's fairly pale in the glass, but there's good intensity of flavour in the wine. On the light side of medium bodied, this pinot is dry with fairly upfront tannins, and shows nicely consistent and layered flavours. The acidity adds freshness. This is a good choice for lighter dishes, such as roast chicken and turkey.

NOTES

....

....

....

....

....

Trius Cabernet Franc 2010

★ ★ ★ ★ ★

VQA NIAGARA PENINSULA $14.95   687964

This is a gorgeous cabernet franc that shows well across the board. The flavours are rich, even plush, with great concentration and complexity, and they're ably supported and complemented by fresh acidity. The tannins are quite firm but quite manageable. The result is a big yet easy-to-drink wine. It goes very well with well-seasoned red meats and other hearty dishes all year round.

NOTES

....

....

....

....

Trius Cabernet Sauvignon 2010

NEW!
★ ★ ★ ★ ½

VQA NIAGARA PENINSULA $14.95   687956

The Trius line from Hillebrand Estates is very good across the board, and this medium-bodied cabernet sauvignon fits effortlessly into the range. It's quite stylish, with concentrated and layered flavours of ripe fruit. The acidity translates as a juicy texture. Dry with firm tannins, it's a great choice for grilled or roasted red meats, and for meat-based or vegetarian stews.

NOTES

....

....

....

....

Trius Merlot 2010

★ ★ ★ ★

VQA NIAGARA PENINSULA $14.95   687907

I wonder how many people realize that Trius is one of Niagara's big success stories. It offers consistent quality at a good price, such that Hillebrand (the producer) added "Trius" in large letters to its roadside signage. This is a lovely, soft-textured merlot with solid, complex flavours and excellent balance. It's dry with moderate tannins, and goes well with grilled or roasted red meats.

NOTES

....

....

....

Trius Red 2010

★ ★ ★ ★ ½

VQA NIAGARA PENINSULA $22.95   303800

[Vintages Essential] Trius Red has been a quality wine ever since it was launched. A blend of cabernet sauvignon, cabernet franc and merlot, it's aged in oak barrels for a year. It's quite delicious, with concentrated and defined flavours, and a generous and tangy texture. Medium bodied and dry, with moderate tannins, it's a natural for red meats and hearty stews.

NOTES

....

....

....

....

....

PORTUGAL

PORTUGAL IS BEST KNOWN FOR PORT, and it seems logical that some of its best red wines are made from grape varieties permitted in port. They tend to be full of flavour, assertive in texture and big bodied. This also means that Portuguese reds are mainly made from indigenous grapes, and producers have generally resisted planting international varieties such as cabernet sauvignon and syrah. Portugal is a good source for inexpensive reds, as the following list shows.

The name of a region following DOC (*Denominação de Origem Controlada*) signifies a designated Portuguese wine region.

NEW!
★ ★ ★ ½

Berço do Infante Reserva 2008

VINHO REGIONAL LISBOA $8.70 253864

Made from the Portuguese varieties castelão and aragonez, this is intensely flavoured, has some complexity and brings enough acidity to the table to provide a quite fresh texture. The tannins are drying and moderate, and it's a good choice for burgers, barbecued ribs and grilled red meats in general.

NOTES

NEW!
★ ★ ★ ★

Catedral Reserva Dão 2008

DOC DÃO $10.95 219816

There's plenty of flavour and a quite rich texture in this affordable blend of alfrocheiro, tinta roriz and touriga nacional (the latter are two of the grape varieties permitted in port). The fruit-acid balance is good, and there's a decent degree of complexity and light tannins. Dry and more than medium bodied, it's a very good choice for well-seasoned, grilled or roasted red meats.

NOTES

NEW!
★ ★ ★ ½

JP Azeitão Red 2011

VINHO REGIONAL PENÍNSULA DE SETÚBAL $8.95 286195

This is another well-priced Portuguese blend, this time from the castelão, aragonez and syrah varieties. It's full of flavour, with good density and some complexity, and the balancing acidity is expressed as an edgy, tangy texture. Try this with burgers, red meats and full-flavoured dishes of many kinds.

NOTES

Quartetto 2008

NEW!
★★★★

VINHO REGIONAL ALENTEJANO $8.70   253880

With a name like Quartetto, you might think this was a blend of four grape varieties. But no, there are three: aragonez, syrah and alicante bouchet. This trio plays well, giving us a red wine with concentrated flavours, a pleasant, tangy, and juicy texture, and a real dryness from the tannins. Make it a quartet by adding food—something like grilled red meat or spicy sausages.

NOTES

....

....

....

....

Veedha Red 2009

NEW!
★★★★

DOC DOURO $12.95   255851

Veedha means "life" in Portuguese, and there is indeed a lot of life in this red blend. Made from tinta roriz, touriga nacional and franca, it delivers concentrated flavours from start to long finish, along with a lively (there it is), fresh and tangy texture. The tannins are there and manageable, and it's a very good choice for richer red meat dishes, hearty stews and well-seasoned dishes of many kinds.

NOTES

....

....

....

....

Vila Regia Reserva 2009

★★★★

DOC DOURO $9.75   613950

This is made from four of the dozens of grape varieties that can be used for making port. It has the characteristic features of red wines from the Douro region (where port comes from): intense flavours, substantial weight, good structure, a mouth-filling texture and drying tannins. It goes well with hearty dishes, so pair it with a winter stew or barbecued red meats.

NOTES

....

....

....

....

SOUTH AFRICA

MOST OF THE WINE REGIONS OF SOUTH AFRICA are warm, and this tends to make for reds that have concentrated flavours and fairly high alcohol. The conditions are right for a wide range of grape varieties. The country's signature red grape is pinotage, a cross of two varieties that was developed there in the 1920s. More popular varieties found in the LCBO are shiraz, merlot and cabernet sauvignon.

Wines from official South African wine regions are called "Wines of Origin." In this list, the initials WO followed by a region indicate where the wine is from.

NEW!
★★★ ½

The Beach House Shiraz/Mourvèdre/Viognier 2010

WO WESTERN CAPE $9.95 223453

These are three grapes from southern France, and they do well in the warm growing conditions of South Africa. Beach House red is a well-made blend that strikes the right note for its price. It shows well-concentrated, solid and modestly complex fruit, and it's nicely balanced, with the fresh acidity contributing tanginess to the texture. Minimally tannic, it makes a good wine for hamburgers and grilled red meats.

NOTES

....

....

....

....

NEW!
★★★★

Boschendahl 'The Pavillion' Shiraz/Cabernet Sauvignon 2010

WO WESTERN CAPE $11.95 222299

This is a well-made red blend that's very versatile with food. You can be equally comfortable serving it on the patio—with burgers and ribs—as at the table—with roasted, braised, grilled or stewed red meats. It shows flavours that are concentrated and nicely layered, good fruit-acid balance, a full and tangy texture and supple, manageable tannins.

NOTES

....

....

....

....

★★★ ½

Durbanville Hills Shiraz 2009

WO DURBANVILLE $11.95 22269

Although Australians grabbed shiraz as their signature wine and made it the big variety success story of the 1990s, they don't have the field entirely to themselves. South Africa produces some notable examples. This one is well made and delivers good fruitiness. Not too complex but flavoursome and nicely balanced, it goes well with burgers and red meat.

NOTES

....

....

....

....

....

Fairview 'Goats Do Roam' 2010

★ ★ ★ ★

WO WESTERN CAPE $12.95   718940

The story goes that the Fairview goats got into the vineyards and ate the best and tastiest fruit. Sounds like they have a great future as consultants. It's also a play on words for the Côtes du Rhône grape varieties (syrah, cinsault, mourvèdre, carignan, grenache) used in the blend. This is consistently well made vintage after vintage, with defined flavours and excellent balance. Drink it with red meats, pork and poultry.

NOTES

....

....

....

....

Nederburg Cabernet Sauvignon 2009

★ ★ ★ ★

WO WESTERN CAPE $10.95   111526

The Nederburg brand dates back two centuries and is one of South Africa's most recognizable names in wine. This cabernet shows that you can produce big volumes (over one million cases a year) and still maintain quality. It's dry and medium bodied, has quite rich flavours and a smooth, mouth-filling, refreshing texture that makes it ideal for food. Drink it with pepper steak or barbecued ribs.

NOTES

....

....

....

....

Nederburg Shiraz 2000

★ ★ ★ ★

WO WESTERN CAPE $10.95   527457

The striking characteristic of this dry, medium-weight shiraz is its balance. You'll find all the concentrated fruit flavours you expect from the variety but, unlike many at this price that are fruity and flat, the texture here is juicy and refreshing. That means it goes especially well with food, and it's versatile enough to handle red meats, veal, pork and poultry.

NOTES

....

....

....

....

SPAIN

SPAIN IS WELL KNOWN for its red wines. Among the many wine regions, Rioja is probably the most recognizable, but you'll find reds from a number of others on this list. Tempranillo is Spain's signature grape variety, and it's the major grape in rioja. But wine is made from many other native and international varieties, especially garnacha (grenache), as this selection shows.

The initials DO (*Denominación de Origen*) indicate a wine from one of Spain's designated wine regions. Two of them, Rioja and Priorat, have been elevated to DOC (*Denominación de Origen Calificada*) level.

NEW!
★★★★

Beso de Vino Syrah/Garnacha 2009

DO CARIÑENA $10.05   231787

This is a big, modern blend that shows intense flavours with some complexity, and well-complemented acidity that comes through as edgy tanginess, verging on juiciness. It's full bodied and moderately tannic, and you can drink it with the full range of grilled game and red meats and heavy winter stews.

NOTES

....

....

....

....

....

★★★★

Campo Viejo Reserva Rioja 2007

DOC RIOJA $17.95   137810

Unlike a generic rioja, a reserva rioja has to age for a specified number of years in barrel and bottle before going on sale. For that reason, reservas tend to have more intensity and complexity . . . as this one does. It delivers quite intense and complex flavours, a rich and tangy texture and good tannic structure. It's medium bodied and dry, and goes well with grilled or roasted red meats, or with meat cooked in red wine.

NOTES

....

....

....

....

★★★★ ½

Campo Viejo Rioja Crianza 2008

DOC RIOJA $12.95   620997

This is a very attractive young rioja. It's medium bodied and displays vibrant, fresh, but nicely layered flavours, and a tangy and refreshing texture. The tannins are firm and drying, but quite manageable. It has the intensity to handle roasted or grilled red meats, but it also has the structure and restraint to go equally well with roast turkey (and the cranberries) or pork.

NOTES

....

....

....

....

Castillo de Almansa Reserva 2008

★ ★ ★ ½

DO ALMANSA $11.95   270363

Almansa is a small wine region not far inland from Spain's Mediterranean coast, where the days get very hot during the growing season. It shows in this wine, which has concentrated and reasonably complex flavours of sweet fruit. It's bone dry and medium bodied, with firm tannins and a tangy texture. It goes very nicely with well-seasoned red meat dishes all year round, and with hearty stews in winter.

NOTES

Castillo de Monséran Garnacha 2010

★ ★ ★ ★

DO CARIÑENA $8.95   73395

This is a basic red that's well priced and great for drinking on the patio when you're serving burgers, ribs and other well-seasoned red meats. Made from the grape variety better known as grenache, it delivers rich and intense sweet fruit flavours with limited complexity, along with a tangy texture. It's medium bodied and negligibly tannic.

NOTES

Corona d'Aragón 'Old Vine' Garnacha 2009

NEW!
★ ★ ★ ★

DO CARIÑENA $12.05   253591

This is a rich, intensely flavoured red that goes well with well-seasoned red meats, but you could keep the Spanish theme and serve it with paella, too. The flavours are deep and plush with good, layered complexity. They're effectively balanced by the acidity, and the tannins are there but manageable.

NOTES

Gran Feudo Reserva 2006

DO NAVARRA $15.75   479014

[Vintages Essential] Made from tempranillo (Spain's signature grape variety), cabernet sauvignon and merlot, this very attractive dry red goes well with all kinds of grilled red meat, as well as hearty stews and risottos, whether or not they feature meat. The fruit is ripe and sweet, with layered complexity, and it's underpinned by refreshing acidity and framed by moderate tannins.

NOTES

....

....

....

....

Las Rocas de San Alejandro Garnacha 2009

DO CALATAYUD $14.95   289977

This is made 100 percent from 80-year-old garnacha (alias grenache). It's said that older vines, with their low fruit yield, produce grapes with more concentration and complexity, and you can taste and feel it here. This is intensely flavoured and solid, right through the palate, and it has the added assets of complexity, balance and (for drinking now) soft tannins. Enjoy it with red meats and hearty casseroles.

NOTES

....

....

....

....

★ ★ ★ ★

Marqués de Cáceres Crianza Rioja 2008

DOC RIOJA $16.95   69294

You never see a crianza from a very recent vintage, because to be labelled "crianza" (matured) a wine must be aged at least three years (spending at least one of those in oak barrels) before being released for sale. This one delivers solid and intense flavours with a hint of oak, and very good balance. It's medium bodied and dry with easygoing tannins. It teams well with a wide range of red meats and hearty pasta dishes.

NOTES

....

....

....

....

Marqués de Riscal Reserva Rioja 2006

★ ★ ★ ★ ½

DOC RIOJA $21.15   32656

Made mainly from the tempranillo variety, with assistance from graciano and mazuelo, this is aged more than two years in oak barrels and a number more in the bottle before you buy it. It's one of the older vintages in the LCBO, and shows ripe, bright and maturing flavours, with fresh acidity and moderate, drying tannins. It's a good choice for paella, red meats, pork and many older, full-flavoured cheeses.

NOTES

....

....

....

....

Montecillo Crianza Rioja 2008

★ ★ ★ ★

DOC RIOJA $14.95   144493

In Spanish wine law, a "crianza" wine has to undergo oak barrel–aging and bottle-aging at the winery. In Rioja, that means at least one year in oak plus two in the bottle before it goes on sale. This example shows quite intense and complex flavours (with definite hints of oak) and a texture that's medium bodied and quite tangy. Drink it with a dish that features meat in a tomato-based sauce.

NOTES

....

....

....

....

Montecillo Reserva Rioja 2006

★ ★ ★ ★ ½

DOC RIOJA $18.45   621003

This is a lovely example of a reserva rioja—aged a minimum time in barrel and bottle, and not sold until four years after vintage. Look for elegance across the board here, with concentrated and layered flavours, very good balance and a smooth, attractive texture. Drink it with red meats, well-seasoned poultry or aged, full-flavour cheeses, such as manchego.

NOTES

....

....

....

....

Muga Reserva Rioja 2007

★ ★ ★ ★ ★

DOC RIOJA $23.95   177345

[Vintages Essential] Muga is an iconic name in Spanish wine, and this rioja is tremendous value. It's a blend of tempranillo (75 percent), grenache (15 percent) and mazuelo graciano (the rest), and it delivers wonderful flavour intensity and complexity. It's very dry and moderately tannic yet light on its feet, and it has the tanginess that suits food. Drink it with grilled red meats and hearty stews.

NOTES

....

....

....

....

Solaz Shiraz/Tempranillo 2009

★ ★ ★ ½

VINO DE LA TIERRA DE CASTILLA $10.95   620922

This blend tastes a lot like many shirazes at this price, with sweet, fruity flavours, but the tempranillo contributes a bit more complexity. It's dry and medium bodied, with a texture that's quite dense and somewhat tannic, but with some juiciness so that it goes well with food. You can drink this with roasted or grilled red meats, burgers or cheeses like cheddar aged three or more years.

NOTES

....

....

....

....

Torres 'Gran Coronas' Cabernet Sauvignon 2006

★ ★ ★ ★ ½

DO PENEDÈS $18.95   36483

[Vintages Essential] Torres is one of the best-known names in Spanish wine, and this cabernet sauvignon (with 15 percent tempranillo blended in to give it some Spanish blood) shows the quality and value that underlie its reputation. The fruit is sweet, ripe, layered and concentrated, and the texture is generous and tangy. It's medium-to-full in body and dry, and has a good tannic grip. Enjoy it with grilled or braised red meats.

NOTES

....

....

....

....

Torres Infinite 2009

NEW!
★ ★ ★ ★

VINO DE LA TIERRA SPAIN $13.00 231795

Mostly (85 percent) tempranillo with some cabernet sauvignon, this is an attractive red that goes well with red meats, pork, rich poultry (like coq au vin) and many paellas. It's quite rich and smooth textured, with concentrated flavours that are consistent right through the palate. Dry and medium weight, it shows very manageable and drying tannins.

NOTES

Torres Sangre de Toro 2009

NEW!
★ ★ ★ ★

DO CATALUNYA $11.95 6585

Each bottle has a little plastic bull hanging off it, in case you're not sure of the meaning of toro. Made from grenache and carignan, this is full of rich flavour. The texture is a little rustic—a good quality—with edgy tanginess and modest tannins. It's dry and medium bodied, and goes very well with red meats, paella, pork and many things from the barbecue.

NOTES

Viña Zaco Tempranillo Rioja 2008

NEW!
★ ★ ★ ★

DOC RIOJA $14.95 243097

This is a well-made, quite juicy red, mostly made from tempranillo, the signature grape of the Rioja region. The flavours are bright but serious and solid right through the palate, and they're paired with a clean, food-friendly seam of acidity. It's dry and lightly tannic, and goes well with a range of foods. Try it with braised pork, red meats, hearty risottos and coq au vin.

NOTES

WASHINGTON STATE

WASHINGTON STATE IS WELL KNOWN for its reds, particularly merlot from the Columbia Valley region. Like other US states, with the obvious exception of California, it is seldom represented on the LCBO's shelves.

14 Hands 'Hot to Trot' Red Blend 2009

WASHINGTON STATE $15.75   226522

Named for the wild horses that used to live in the hills of Washington State, this blend brings together merlot, syrah and cabernet sauvignon, with a dash of mourvèdre and some other red varieties. It's intensely flavoured with good, layered complexity, and has a nice seam of clean acidity to keep the fruit honest. It's a very good choice for red meats, as well as burgers and ribs.

NOTES

....

....

....

....

ROSÉS

ROSÉ WINE HAS ENJOYED A RENAISSANCE in the last couple of years. Until recently, too many were sweet and simple—fine for everyday drinking, but not particularly complex or interesting. Things have changed, though, and rosé has become a popular style, leading producers to make more and more that are well balanced and structured. There are more dry rosés now, along with well-made sweeter styles, and producers have begun to show the varieties, just as they do for whites and reds.

Beginning in spring, the LCBO releases a large number of rosés for the warm months, when demand is highest. But rosés make good drinking all year round.

Cave Spring Rosé 2011

★ ★ ★ ★

VQA NIAGARA ESCARPMENT, ONTARIO $14.95   295006

Today many winemakers are trying to make "serious" rosés, which are too often reds in all but colour. Taste them blind and you'd think you were drinking red wine. This rosé, made from cabernet franc (82 percent) and cabernet sauvignon (18 percent), is in a more familiar style, with vibrant, fresh, fruity flavours. It's dry and medium weight with a crisp, clean texture. It goes well with roast ham or turkey, or summer salads.

NOTES

Gallo White Zinfandel 2010

NEW!
★ ★ ★ ½

CALIFORNIA $8.95   285767

White zinfandel is often sneered at as an inferior style, but Americans buy about 200 million bottles of it a year. This is a popular brand that shows the bright, quite sweet fruit flavours typical of the style, along with good, crisp acidity. Chill it down and sip it on its own, or drink it with summer salads, spicy Asian dishes or barbecued meats with a sweet, tangy sauce.

NOTES

Gran Feudo Rosado 2010

NEW!
★ ★ ★ ★

DO NAVARRA, SPAIN $11.95   165845

This rosé is made mainly from the garnacha tinta (black grenache) variety. After the grapes are pressed, the juice is left on the skins for 24 hours, just long enough for them to make the juice a bright pink colour. Apart from the hue, the texture and flavours are also attractive. It's a mid-weight, dry, well-balanced rosé with good concentration and focus, and it goes well—all year round—with white fish and many poultry dishes.

NOTES

Malivoire 'LadyBug' Rosé 2010

NEW!
★ ★ ★ ★ ½

VQA NIAGARA PENINSULA, ONTARIO $15.95   659088

[Vintages Essential] Malivoire's 'LadyBug' rosé, a blend of cabernet franc, gamay and pinot noir, has been a hit for more than ten years. One of the earliest of a new generation of rosés, it's dry and full bodied, but it's definitively a rosé, not a red in pink clothing. Look for a great fruit-acid balance, and enjoy this with baked ham or roasted poultry.

NOTES
....
....
....
....
....

Ogier Ventoux Rosé 2010

★ ★ ★ ½

AOC VENTOUX, FRANCE $10.95   134916

A blend of grenache, syrah and cinsault from the south of France, this is a dry rosé that drinks well on its own, and also pairs well with summer salads and roast chicken. Look for bright, nicely concentrated flavours, paired with good acidity that translates to a crisp, clean texture.

NOTES
....
....
....
....
....
....

Rémy Pannier Rosé d'Anjou 2010

★ ★ ★ ½

AOC ROSÉ D'ANJOU, FRANCE $11.95   12641

This rosé gets its colour from cabernet franc, but don't be fooled by the paleness of its hue. The flavours are quite concentrated, and it has a crisp texture that suits it for drinking on its own or with food. It goes well with summer salads, but is a year-round pairing with the likes of roast poultry.

NOTES
....
....
....
....

SPARKLING WINES
& CHAMPAGNES

HERE'S THE DIFFERENCE between champagne and sparkling wine: All champagnes are sparkling wines, but not all sparkling wines are champagnes. Champagne is a sparkling wine made in the Champagne region of France, from specified grape varieties and in a method strictly defined by wine law. Sparkling wines made elsewhere cannot be called champagne—even if they're made from the same grape varieties and by the same method.

In line with changing tastes, more and more restaurants offer sparkling wine by the glass, to drink either as an aperitif or with meals. Dry sparkling wine goes well with many dishes, such as fish, seafood, poultry and pork. Fruitier or off-dry styles are excellent with spicy dishes, such as much Asian cuisine, with which you might otherwise drink beer.

Sparkling wine has been made for centuries, but there's no clear answer to the question of where or when it was made first. A credible claim comes from Limoux, in southwest France, where it seems to have been made in the 1500s and where a sparkling wine called Blanquette de Limoux is now made. Sparkling wine was popularized by producers in France's Champagne region, where sparkling wine was first made in the late 1600s by a monk called Dom Pérignon.

Much of the Dom Pérignon story is myth, but there's no doubt about the success of champagne. It was aggressively marketed in the 1800s and became associated with special events of all kinds. Generations later, champagne continues to feature at celebrations as varied as ship launchings, Grand Prix victories and weddings.

But although it has become the brand name for sparkling wine, only some sparkling wine is genuine champagne. To be labelled as such, the wine has to be made using specific grape varieties from vineyards in the Champagne region of northeast France according to a specific method. That method involves adding sugar and alcohol to base wine and allowing a second fermentation to occur in the bottle that is sold to the consumer. This procedure is known variously as the champagne method, traditional method or classic method (and their French translations).

Even when they use the specified grape varieties and employ the champagne method, producers elsewhere are not permitted to label their wines "champagne." In fact, they can't describe the wine as being made by the champagne method and must use an alternative term. Sparkling wine can be produced using other methods, too, and many (but not all) of the less expensive sparkling wines are made using techniques that are less costly and time-consuming. One involves a second fermentation in a tank, with the sparkling wine being bottled under pressure. Another involves carbonating wine in the same way as soft drinks.

Apart from champagne, there are several other common categories of sparkling wine: cava, prosecco and crémant.

- CAVA (which means "cellar") is made in the northeast of Spain according to the same method used in making champagne, but generally using grape varieties native to Spain.
- PROSECCO is an Italian sparkling wine made from the glera grape variety. It tends to be fruitier than cava and champagn e.
- CRÉMANT is a category comprising wines from French regions, such as Crémant de Bourgogne and Crémant de Loire, made according to the same method used in making champagne.

Some other terms you find on labels of sparkling wine refer to dryness, which is based on the amount of residual sugar in the wine. Most sparkling wines are labelled "brut," which means they taste dry. "Extra brut" means they are even drier, while wines labelled "sec" are a little sweeter.

Unlike most still wines, sparkling wines are generally non-vintage and don't show a year on their label. This is because the base wine used for making sparkling wine is usually drawn from several vintages. Vintage-dated sparkling wines do exist, but they tend to be more expensive, especially vintage champagne.

A word of caution: Sparkling wine is under pressure, and you should take care not to let the cork shoot out of the bottle; it can seriously injure you or someone else. Always keep your thumb on the cork as you remove the foil and wire cage. Open the bottle by holding the cork and twisting the bottle, not vice versa. You can also hold a cloth, like a tea towel, over the cork to make sure it doesn't escape. Ease the cork from the bottle so that you hear a gentle hiss, rather than a loud pop.

The following list of best-value sparkling wines carried by the LCBO is divided into two categories: sparkling wines and champagnes.

SPARKLING WINES

NEW!
★★★★

Astoria Extra Dry Prosecco

DOC PROSECCO, ITALY $13.95   693855

[Non-vintage] Prosecco is a grape variety, but because it also became widely used to refer to the sparkling wine, an alternative name of the grape—glera—has been adopted to avoid confusion. Prosecco tends to be fruity and easy drinking, but some (like this one) show superior structure and balance. It's ideal for sipping before a meal, but you can also serve it with spicy food, as the sparkling fruitiness will help tone down the heat.

NOTES

....
....
....

NEW!
★★★ ½

The Beach House Sparkling Wine

WO WESTERN CAPE, SOUTH AFRICA $12.95   299799

[Non-vintage] This sparkler is made from the chenin blanc variety, which is used to make sparkling wine in France's Loire Valley. Here, though, it's made in a much fruitier, easy-drinking style. The flavours are bright and vibrant, and there's a good seam of acidity, but there's little of the acid bite you find in some sparkling wines. Drink this on its own (it has only 8 percent alcohol, so it's great for summer) or with spicy barbecued seafood.

NOTES

....
....
....
....

★★★★

Bottega Il Vino dei Poeti Prosecco

DOC PROSECCO, ITALY $13.70   897702

[Non-vintage] Bottega is one of the prime producers of prosecco, and you'll easily recognize this wine by its black and gold label. The wine inside is easy drinking and fruity with just a hint of sweetness. It's crisp and clean in texture and leaves your palate feeling refreshed. It's ideal as an aperitif or with spicy appetizers.

NOTES

....
....
....
....

Cave Spring 'Blanc de Blancs' Brut Sparkling Wine

NEW!
★ ★ ★ ★ ½

VQA NIAGARA ESCARPMENT, ONTARIO $29.95 213983

[Non-vintage] This lovely bottle of bubbles was made from chardonnay grapes (hence the reference to white grapes in 'Blanc de Blancs') in the traditional method used for champagne. It shows stylish fruit that's defined and focused, supported by well-calibrated acidity and enhanced by the streams of fine bubbles. It's fine drinking on its own or with seafood, shellfish, fish, poultry and pork.

NOTES

....

....

....

....

Château de Montgueret Crémant de Loire Brut

NEW!
★ ★ ★ ★

AOC CRÉMANT DE LOIRE, FRANCE $18.95 217760

[Non-vintage] This sparkling wine is made the same way as champagne. It's a lovely blend of chenin blanc, chardonnay and cabernet franc. Slightly off-dry, with attractive and complex flavours, it's an excellent aperitif that will perk up your appetite. Or pair it with spicy Asian dishes, especially seafood like garlic and ginger shrimp.

NOTES

....

....

....

....

Château des Charmes Brut Sparkling Wine

★ ★ ★ ★

VQA NIAGARA-ON-THE-LAKE, ONTARIO $22.95 145409

[Non-vintage] Made from chardonnay and pinot noir, and in the traditional method developed in Champagne, this is a lovely dry sparkling wine that delivers quality from start to finish. The flavours are pungent and nuanced, with good concentration, and the acidity is bright and correct. There are plenty of bubbles, contributing to a finely grained, crisp mousse. Drink it on its own or with poultry, pork, white fish, seafood or smoked salmon.

NOTES

....

....

....

Codorníu Brut Classico Cava
NEW!
★ ★ ★ ★ ½

DO CAVA, SPAIN $12.75   215814

[Non-vintage] Cava is made in the same way as champagne, which is to say that it goes through a fermentation in the actual bottle you buy (rather than being bottled after the fermentation is complete). This is a very attractive example, with great flavours and a lovely crisp and balanced texture. It has plenty of small bubbles and a soft mousse. Sip it on its own or serve it with spicy chicken, pork or seafood.

NOTES

....

....

....

....

De Chanceny Crémant de Loire Brut Rosé
NEW!
★ ★ ★ ★

AOC CRÉMANT DE LOIRE, FRANCE $16.65   211466

[Non-vintage] "Crémant" indicates a sparkling wine from one of a number of French wine regions. This one, a rosé, is from the Loire Valley, where it's made from cabernet franc, and shows lively fruit flavours. The texture is crisp and clean and the bubbles are plentiful. This makes a fine sparkler to drink on its own, and it also goes well with roast turkey and cranberries.

NOTES

....

....

....

....

Freixenet 'Cordon Negro' Brut Cava
★ ★ ★ ★

DO CAVA, SPAIN $13.95   216945

[Non-vintage] This is one of those reliable, versatile sparkling wines that you can count on, batch after batch. A blend of three grape varieties indigenous to Spain, and made in the same way as champagne (it was fermented in the bottle you buy), it delivers lovely vibrant fruit flavours, and has a zesty and refreshing texture. It has all the fizz you want for a special occasion, for an aperitif or for a spicy Asian dish.

NOTES

....

....

....

....

★ ★ ★ ★

Freixenet 'Cordon Rosado' Brut Cava

DO CAVA, SPAIN $12.95   217059

[Non-vintage] This is a rosé sparkling wine that makes a pretty addition to a summer table; it also works well on a winter table as a reminder that summer will eventually return. It has bright, ripe, sweet fruit flavours, but the wine itself is bone dry. The texture is crisp and refreshing, and the bubbles are plentiful and create a lovely mousse. This is perfect with a summer salad, but you can also serve it with baked ham or roasted chicken.

NOTES

....

....

....

★ ★ ★ ★ ½

Henry of Pelham 'Cuvée Catharine' Brut Sparkling Wine

VQA NIAGARA PENINSULA, ONTARIO $29.95   217505

[Non-vintage] Made from chardonnay and pinot noir, the two varieties most often used in champagne, this sparkling wine is dry, crisp and compelling. The flavours are layered and defined, with a complex profile, and they're lifted by the vibrant acidity and steady streams of fine bubbles. The mousse is clean and crisp. This is great with oysters, shellfish and seafood in general, or as a partner to pork or white fish.

NOTES

....

....

....

....

★ ★ ★ ★ ½

Henry of Pelham 'Cuvée Catharine' Rosé Brut Sparkling Wine

VQA NIAGARA PENINSULA, ONTARIO $29.95   217521

[Non-vintage] This is a lovely sparkling rosé made from chardonnay and pinot noir by the method used in champagne (although the label can't express it in that way). You'll find very attractive, vibrant fruit flavours here, and they're echoed by the crisp, refreshing texture and fine bubbles. This is a lovely wine for the summer (or winter) table, and it's great for roast turkey, salads and spicy dishes featuring chicken and seafood.

NOTES

....

....

....

Jacob's Creek 'Brut Cuvée'
Chardonnay/Pinot Noir Sparkling Wine

★ ★ ★ ★

AUSTRALIA $14.25   210633

[Non-vintage] This wine is made using the same method as champagne, and from the same two main grape varieties. It's a very good choice as an aperitif, and it has the weight to go with many meat or pasta dishes prepared in a creamy sauce. You'll find it has well-defined flavours and a substantial and crisp texture, and it forms a very pleasant mousse in your mouth.

NOTES

....

....

....

Mumm Cuvée Napa 'Brut Prestige' Sparkling Wine

★ ★ ★ ★

NAPA VALLEY, CALIFORNIA $28.25   217273

[Non-vintage] French fizz tradition comes to California in this sparkling wine made in Napa (using the same grape varieties—pinot noir, chardonnay and pinot meunier—as in champagne) by a famous champagne house. This is a great sparkling wine to drink as an aperitif—it has the crisp, mouth-watering texture that sets you up for food—or to enjoy with oysters. The flavours are complex and nuanced, the mousse is soft and defined.

NOTES

....

....

....

Paul Delane Réserve Brut Crémant de Bourgogne

NEW!
★ ★ ★ ★

AOC CRÉMANT DE BOURGOGNE, FRANCE $17.30   214981

[Non-vintage] This nicely balanced sparkling wine is made from four of Burgundy's permitted varieties: pinot noir, gamay, chardonnay and aligoté. It has a crisp and clean texture from the bright acidity, concentrated flavours and streams of bubbles that end in a good mousse. Sip it on its own or drink it with grilled seafood, smoked salmon or many spicy Asian dishes.

NOTES

....

....

....

....

Peller Estate 'Classic' Ice Cuvée

NEW!
★★★★

VQA NIAGARA PENINSULA, ONTARIO $31.95   216127

[Non-vintage] This is an original Canadian sparkling wine. When sparkling wine is made by the method perfected in Champagne, a dosage of sugar is added to spark a second fermentation in the bottle. Here, the dosage is sugar-rich icewine. You get the refreshing vibrancy of sparkling wine, with an added dimension of flavour and fruitiness (but not the sweetness) from the icewine. Drink it on its own or with spicy Asian dishes.

NOTES

....

....

....

Santa Margherita Valdobbiadene Prosecco Superiore

NEW!
★★★★ ½

DOCG VALDOBBIADENE PROSECCOR SUPERIORE, ITALY

$17.95   687582

[Non-vintage][Vintages Essential] Made in a brut (dry) style, this prosecco is a cut above many of its kind. It has the fruit richness of many proseccos, but it's a lot drier than most and shows more structure and complexity. You can drink this on its own or as an aperitif, or pair it with a broad spectrum of foods, from seafood, fish and poultry to pork and spicy Asian dishes.

NOTES

....

....

....

Segura Viudas Brut Reserva Cava

NEW!
★★★★

DO CAVA, SPAIN $14.35   216960

[Non-vintage] Made by the same method as champagne, but from different grape varieties, this sparkling wine offers lovely, concentrated flavours and brisk acidity. You'll find streams of bubbles and a soft, attractive mousse. Like many dry sparkling wines, it's extremely versatile on the table, and you can pair it with poultry, seafood, fish and spicy dishes (like many curries). Or serve it off the table as a wine to sip on its own.

NOTES

....

....

....

....

Toso Malbec Rosé Brut Sparkling Wine

NEW!
★ ★ ★ ½

MENDOZA, ARGENTINA $14.95   162628

[Non-vintage] This is a straightforward, uncomplicated sparkling rosé that's great for sipping on its own. It also goes well with roasted chicken or turkey, baked ham and many salads. The flavours are nicely concentrated and the balance is good, making for a clean, flavourful and refreshing sparkler that shows decent bubbles and mousse.

NOTES

Trius Brut Sparkling Wine

★ ★ ★ ★

NIAGARA PENINSULA, ONTARIO $24.95   215913

[Non-vintage] This Niagara sparkling wine is made from chardonnay and pinot noir grapes and fermented according to the method used for champagne (what is often called the classic or traditional method). It's a very well-balanced wine, with lovely, well-defined fruit flavours complemented by a clean and crisp texture. The mousse is soft and the bubbles are small, and it's an excellent party or aperitif sparkler.

NOTES

Wolf Blass 'Yellow Label' Sparkling Brut

★ ★ ★ ½

SOUTH EASTERN AUSTRALIA $17.95   649996

[Non-vintage] This is another of those well-made, good-value, versatile sparkling wines that you can sip on its own, mix with orange or other juice, or drink with appetizers or main courses. The secret is in the balance—and you have it here—between good, solid fruit flavours and crisp, refreshing texture. If you're planning to drink this with food, think of fairly rich chicken, pork or turkey dishes.

NOTES

CHAMPAGNES

★ ★ ★ ★ ½ **Lanson 'Black Label' Brut Champagne**

AOC CHAMPAGNE $49.85   41889

[Non-vintage] This is a delightfully complex champagne at the less expensive end of the price spectrum. The flavours are well defined, and it's crisp and clean with a soft mousse (the froth that forms in your mouth). Look at the bubbles in your glass and you'll see they form vertical lines, a sign of a good-quality champagne. Drink this as an aperitif or with seafood, fish, pork or spicy dishes.

NOTES

....

....

NEW!
★ ★ ★ ★   **Mumm 'Carte Classique' Extra Dry Champagne**

AOC CHAMPAGNE $59.95   308064

[Non-vintage] In the crazy language of wine, extra dry is not as dry as brut. It's sort of middling dry, as distinct from very dry, and many people prefer the softer texture of extra dry when they're looking for a champagne to drink on its own. This is a very good choice. It presents lovely fruit flavours, good, clean acidity and a soft but defined mousse. And, of course, you can pair it with food, too!

NOTES

....

....

....

....

★ ★ ★ ★   **Mumm 'Cordon Rouge' Brut Champagne**

AOC CHAMPAGNE $59.95   308056

[Non-vintage] You could serve this on Mother's Day, but the Mumm here is pronounced MOOM, as in "moon." It's one of the best-known champagnes, and you can't miss its diagonal red stripe (the "cordon rouge") on the shelf in the LCBO. It's just well made, with all the crispness you want from champagne, not to mention the nuanced flavours. With a soft mousse and good weight, it goes well with chicken, turkey or rich fish dishes.

NOTES

....

....

....

....

★ ★ ★ ★

Nicolas Feuillatte 'Réserve Particulière' Brut Champagne

AOC CHAMPAGNE $44.30   637605

[Non-vintage] This is an attractive champagne from start to finish. Pour it and watch the streams of bubbles, then sip it and appreciate the zestiness of the first mouthful and the creamy mousse it forms. With complex, well-defined flavours, this makes an excellent aperitif, but also carries through to the table and goes well with rich chicken dishes.

NOTES

....

....

....

....

....

NEW!
★ ★ ★ ★

Nicolas Feuillatte 'Réserve Particulière' Brut Rosé Champagne

AOC CHAMPAGNE $56.95   267039

[Non-vintage] Rosé champagnes are on a roll, with more and more champagne houses producing pink versions of their classics. This one shows bright, vibrant fruit flavours, zesty acidity, plenty of fine bubbles and a soft mousse. The colour, which is more salmon-bronze than pink, adds to your table. This wine is delicious on its own or with dishes like melon and prosciutto and sautéed shrimps.

NOTES

....

....

....

NEW!
★ ★ ★ ★ ½

Perrier-Jouet 'Grand Brut' Brut Champagne

AOC CHAMPAGNE $64.95   155341

[Non-vintage] This is a really lovely champagne that sizzles on its own or in the company of food. The flavours are rich, tiered and well focused, and the texture is crisp and elegant. Here you find a winning tension between the brisk acidity and the roundness of the fruit, with hints of lees flickering between. This is a fine aperitif, and it goes well with many seafood, fish, poultry and pork dishes.

NOTES

....

....

....

....

★ ★ ★ ★

Piper-Heidsieck Brut Champagne

AOC CHAMPAGNE $49.95   462432

[Non-vintage] This is a champagne that's versatile. You can pop the cork (not literally—always ease the cork from a bottle of sparkling wine, so that it opens with a gentle hiss, not a pop) to celebrate birthdays and the like, or serve it with chicken, turkey or pork. Dry and medium bodied, with solid, complex flavours and a refreshing texture, it shows fine streams of bubbles that make for a clean, crisp mousse.

NOTES

....

....

....

....

★ ★ ★ ★ ½

Pol Roger 'Extra Cuvée de Réserve' Brut Champagne

AOC CHAMPAGNE $59.75   217158

[Non-vintage] This is a very good-quality champagne at a very good price. It has everything you look for in the animal: solid fruit flavours, complexity, a crisp and zesty texture, lots of fine bubbles streaming up from the bottom of the glass and an edgy but quite soft mousse in the mouth. It's ideal as an aperitif, but you can take it to the table and drink it with Asian cuisine, seafood, fish, poultry and pork dishes.

NOTES

....

....

....

....

★ ★ ★ ★

Veuve Clicquot-Ponsardin Brut Champagne

AOC CHAMPAGNE $66.35   663338

[Non-vintage] Named for the woman who not only took over production but improved it after her champagne-producer husband died, this has become an iconic champagne. The stylish yellow-orange label stands out on the shelf. The champagne itself is a byword for balance, with well-defined flavours, a crisp, refreshing texture, and fine bubbles and mousse. You can drink this on its own or with smoked salmon, chicken or pork.

NOTES

....

....

....

SWEET &
DESSERT WINES

ALL DESSERT WINES ARE SWEET, but not all sweet wines are suitable for dessert. For example, icewine, which is a style Ontario is famous for, is often too sweet for desserts but goes well with foie gras (which is normally served as an appetizer or part of a main course) and blue cheese. This list includes a number of sweet wines, and I've suggested what goes best with each.

Batasiolo 'Bosc dla Rei' Moscato d'Asti 2011

NEW!
★ ★ ★ ★

DOCG MOSCATO D'ASTI, ITALY $14.95   277194

Made from the moscato variety, this is a luscious, moderately sweet wine that goes well with cheesecakes and fruit pies that are fairly but not too sweet. It has a round texture allied to good acidity, and is very lightly viscous. It would also go well with foie gras and with a cheese course that included not-too-strong blue cheeses.

NOTES
....
....
....

★ ★ ★ ★ ½

Cave Spring 'Indian Summer' Select Late Harvest Riesling 2010

VQA NIAGARA PENINSULA $24.95   415901

[Vintages Essential, 375 mL] This is not icewine, although the grapes were partly frozen when picked. They were left on the vine past the usual harvest date to shrivel and lose water, and then picked after the first frost. The result is a wine with sweet—but not very sweet—flavours that are complex and delicious, complemented by vibrant acidity. It's lovely to drink by itself, but you can serve it (chilled) with any fruit-based dessert that's no sweeter than the wine.

NOTES
....
....
....

★ ★ ★ ★ ★

Henry of Pelham Riesling Icewine 2010

VQA SHORT HILLS BENCH $49.95   430561

[Vintages Essential, 375 mL] This is an icewine that delivers the best in the style. It has all the sweetness that shrivelled and frozen grapes can produce, but it's nuanced and layered. Meanwhile, the threat of a cloying, teeth-hurting experience is averted by the nice line of acidity. It's a more drinkable icewine than many, and for this reason you could chill it slightly (about 15 minutes in the fridge), then sip it by itself or drink it with foie gras or briny blue cheese.

NOTES
....
....
....
....

NEW!
★ ★ ★ ★ ½

Henry of Pelham Special Select Late Harvest Vidal 2010

VQA ONTARIO $19.95   325228

[375 mL] This stylish wine is made using selected vidal grapes from bunches left on the vines well after the normal harvest period. With concentrated sugar, they have produced a luscious wine that goes well with sweet, fruit-based desserts, with briny blue cheese or with seared foie gras. The dense and focused sweet flavours are balanced by brisk and vibrant acidity that cuts through the sweetness and ensures it's not cloying.

NOTES

....

....

....

....

NEW!
★ ★ ★ ★

Inniskillin Vidal Icewine 2008

VQA NIAGARA PENINSULA $49.95   651085

[Vintages Essential, 375 mL] Inniskillin is arguably the world's best-known icewine producer. They make icewine from a number of grape varieties, and this vidal version delivers all the rich, pungent sweetness you buy icewine for, effectively offset by a seam of vibrant acidity. It gives the wine a sort of juiciness that enables you to enjoy it on its own, with blue cheese or with foie gras.

NOTES

....

....

....

....

★ ★ ★ ★

Jackson-Triggs Vidal Icewine 2007

VQA NIAGARA PENINSULA $39.95   694010

[Vintages Essential, 375 mL] Icewine is now made from a wide range of grape varieties—including red—and there are also sparkling icewines, but the majority are made from riesling and vidal. This vidal is sweet to be sure (and icewine couldn't not be), but it's fruity and fairly light on its feet for a medium-to-full-bodied wine. The acidity is clean and balancing, and you can drink this with not-too-sweet, fruit-based desserts or blue cheese.

NOTES

....

....

....

....

Lakeview Cellars Vidal Icewine 2010

★ ★ ★ ½

VQA NIAGARA PENINSULA$19.95622672

[Vintages Essential, 200 mL] The 200 mL bottle is an excellent size—about half the size of a normal bottle of icewine—and it serves four to six people comfortably. This rich example is full bodied and full of luscious, opulent flavours, but it has the necessary seam of acidity in the texture to tame the sweetness. Chill it and drink it on its own or with orange-infused crème brûlée.

NOTES

....

....

....

....

Peller Estates 'Private Reserve' Vidal Icewine 2010

★ ★ ★ ★

VQA NIAGARA PENINSULA$26.9518564

[Vintages Essential, 200 mL] The 200 mL format is very attractive because icewine is a fairly expensive luxury for many people, and a little of it goes a long way. This one is nicely made, with all the luscious sweetness you want plus good structure and complexity. The acidity cuts through effectively, making this a good choice for sweet desserts, blue cheese and foie gras.

NOTES

....

....

....

....

Southbrook Framboise

★ ★ ★ ★ ½

ONTARIO$15.95341024

[Non-vintage, 375 mL] This is the only fruit wine (non-grape wine) in the book. Southbrook's Framboise, made from the royalty variety of raspberries and fortified with a little brandy, has become an icon, and so it's here. It's full of rich, intense, sweet flavours, and the viscous texture has the acidity to cut through the sweetness. Drink it with rich chocolate desserts or pour it over ice cream. Amazing!

NOTES

....

....

....

....

Strewn Select Late Harvest Vidal 2008

★ ★ ★ ★

VQA ONTARIO $15.95   107219

[375 mL] Select late-harvest wines are made from selected grapes picked late in the fall, after the normal harvest. By then, they have started to lose water and to shrivel, concentrating the sugar and producing more sweetness, although not nearly as much as in icewine. This is a very good example, with light viscosity, complex flavours and good acidity. It goes well with blue cheese and with sweet desserts (but make sure they're not as sweet as the wine).

NOTES

....

....

....

....

FORTIFIED WINES

FORTIFIED WINES ARE WINES whose alcohol level has been raised, and style modified, by the addition of brandy or a neutral, distilled alcohol. The best known fortified wines are port and sherry.

Port is a sweet, fortified wine (usually red, sometimes white) made in the Douro region of Portugal. It's generally served after dinner with dessert, cheese, nuts or on its own, and some people like the combination of port and a cigar. Port can also be served as an aperitif, a common practice in France. Although other countries produce fortified wines labelled "port," the name is properly reserved for the wine produced in the Douro region according to the rules set out for port production there.

Sherry is a fortified wine made in Jerez, a wine region in the south of Spain. It comes in many styles—from clear, crisp, light and dry, to black, heavy, viscous and sweet. You'll find other fortified wines labelled "sherry," but only fortified wine from the Jerez region made in a designated way can properly be called sherry. Although sherry is fortified, and is generally drunk as an aperitif, it is also a very successful partner for food, and the spectrum of styles is broad enough that it's possible to find a sherry for any dish.

PORTS

★ ★ ★ ★ ½ **Ferreira 'Dona Antonia Reserva' Port**
DOC PORTO $19.00   157586

[Non-vintage] Named for the head of the Ferreira port-producing family in the early nineteenth century, this is a luscious port. It delivers sweet, rich, multi-layered flavours, and a texture that's quite viscous and seems to swell in your mouth. But the acidity clicks in and kills the sweetness, leaving you with a fruity and complex finish. It's delicious on its own or with blue cheese and roasted nuts.

NOTES

....

....

....

★ ★ ★ ★ ½ **Graham's 10-Year Tawny Port**
DOC PORTO $27.95   206508

[Non-vintage] This is a luscious tawny port, so called for the golden-brown colour it achieves from oxidation and being stored in barrels. This is medium on the sweetness scale, with loads of complexity in the flavour profile. It's a little viscous, has good acid balance and drinks well on its own. If you prefer, you can drink it with bitter chocolate or with briny blue cheeses.

NOTES

....

....

....

★ ★ ★ ★ ½ **Graham's 20-Year Tawny Port**
DOC PORTO $36.95   620641

[Non-vintage, 500 mL] To be labelled as "10-Year" or "20-Year," ports don't actually need to spend that long in oak barrels; they need to achieve the quality and style a port typically would, if it did. But these ports do have long aging, and this one shows it in its structure and in the complexity and depth of its flavours. It's elegant and smooth, and is best appreciated on its own, at least for the first few sips. Then bring on the Stilton.

NOTES

....

....

....

....

NEW!
★ ★ ★ ★
Sandeman Late Bottled Vintage Port 2007
DOC PORTO $16.75   195974

True to its name, this port from the 2007 vintage was bottled in 2011.
It's a classic LBV, with depth and intensity of flavour and texture. Lightly
viscous, it shows plenty of complexity as it moves through the palate, and
is well balanced and nicely tannic. Port is one of the rare wines that go
with chocolate (dark and bitter), so indulge!

NOTES

....

....

....

....

....

NEW!
★ ★ ★ ★ ★
Sandeman 'Vau Vintage' Vintage Port 2000
DOC PORTO $19.95   251090

This is a great price for this vintage port, which is sourced mainly from
the Quinta do Vau vineyard. Look for a really opulent texture here,
somewhat viscous but plush and smooth, carrying flavours that are rich,
sweet and layered. The tannins are well integrated and the acidity is right.
It's a delicious experience on its own, and it can be paired with aged
Stilton (or an equivalent aged cheese) or dark, dark chocolate.

NOTES

....

....

....

....

★ ★ ★ ★ ½
Taylor Fladgate 'First Estate' Reserve Port
DOC PORTO $15.95   309401

[Non-vintage] This is made in a slightly less-sweet style than most ports.
There are some red wines described as port-like because they're so rich,
intense and sweet, and if you think of those, this port is just across the line,
in a style approaching red wine. Being less sweet, it's easier drinking and
goes well with aged cheeses (like very old, crumbly cheddar). The texture
here is intense and rich, but it leaves a drying sensation in your mouth.

NOTES

....

....

....

Warre's 'Otima' 10-Year-Old Port

★ ★ ★ ★

DOC PORTO $21.95   666174

[Non-vintage, 500 mL] If you think of port as an after-dinner drink with the colour and weight of the leather armchairs of the crusty old guys who drink it, try Otima. It's made in a lighter style—as you might expect from the colour of this port, which is paler than most—but it still has lovely, sweet fruit flavours. You can chill it as an aperitif or drink it at room temperature after dinner.

NOTES

....

....

....

....

Alvear Fino Montilla

★ ★ ★ ½

DOC MONTILLA-MORILES $10.95 112771

[Non-vintage] This isn't technically sherry, as it isn't made in Jerez, in southern Spain. Montilla, the region next to Jerez, produces wines in the same styles as sherry, from delicate and bone dry to rich and sweet. This fino (essentially, dry) Montilla is on the delicate and dry end of the spectrum. It's crisp and refreshing, with a light body, and it goes well with salty Spanish tapas like olives and grilled octopus.

NOTES

Harvey's Bristol Cream Sherry

★ ★ ★ ★

DO JEREZ $14.75 215483

[Non-vintage] Some people think of sweet sherry as an old-timers' drink, the sort of thing your grandmother might sip a few clandestine glasses of. But Harvey's Bristol Cream is a delicious, lightly viscous sherry that displays many appealing flavours. Chill it down and you can sip it on its own or with crème caramel. Or try it as a refreshing summer aperitif—on the rocks with a slice of orange.

NOTES

Tio Pepe Extra Dry Fino Sherry

NEW!
★ ★ ★ ★ ½

DO JEREZ $15.95 231829

[Non-vintage] Tio Pepe is an iconic fino sherry, and it's great to have it back in the LCBO. This is an astringently dry style ("extra dry" isn't an exaggeration!) and it has pungent, high-toned flavours backed by high, taut acidity. It's not to everyone's taste when drunk on its own, but it's an excellent partner for many Spanish tapas dishes, such as olives, almonds, grilled octopus and spicy sausage.

NOTES

INDEX

This index includes the grape varieties and blends of varieties as declared on the label of each wine.

Viognier
    Cono Sur, **40**; Baron Philippe de
      Rothschild, **45**; Domaine des
      Aspes, **46**

Z

Zinfandel
    Cline, **125**; Dancing Bull 'Vintage
      Blend', **126**; Deep Purple, **126**;
      Ravenswood 'Old Vines Vintner's
      Blend', **129**; Sledgehammer, **132**;
      Smoking Loon 'Old Vine', **132**;
      Gallo White, **217**
Zweigelt
    Zvy-gelt, **119**

ABOUT THE AUTHOR

Rod Phillips is a wine author, journalist and judge who lives in Ottawa. He is wine columnist for the *Ottawa Citizen* and wine writer and contributing editor of *NUVO* magazine. He contributes to newspapers, magazines, podcasts and other wine media in Canada, the US, Europe and Asia. He writes regularly for *Vines* and *Wine Access*, Canada's leading wine magazines, and has written extensively for *The World of Fine Wine* (UK). He also contributes a regular column to the website of the Guild of Sommeliers (US). In addition, he is the wine advisor to the Ottawa Wine & Food Festival, and co-chair of the Ottawa Wine Challenge.

Apart from the book series *The 500 Best-Value Wines in the LCBO*, Rod has written two books on wine, has judged wine competitions in Canada, Europe, South America and New Zealand, is a member of the CBC Radio Ottawa wine panel and gives wine classes. He was the curator of an exhibition on the history of Canadian wine at the Canadian Museum of Civilization from 2004 to 2005, and he was named Wine Journalist of the Year at the 2007 Ontario Wine Awards. He regularly visits wine regions and wineries around the world.

Rod publishes the *Winepointer* biweekly newsletter, which reviews new wines in the LCBO, Vintages and other places that wine is available in Ontario. You can subscribe to these newsletters for free on his website (rodphillipsonwine.com). You can also read his wine blog on the *Ottawa Citizen*'s website (ottawacitizen.com), follow him on Twitter at @rodphillipswine and contact him at rod@rodphillipsonwine.com.